Günter Grass

Katz und Maus

Noel L. Thomas

Professor of German,
University of Salford.

J. M. Loughridge

April 13th. 1994.

UNIVERSITY OF GLASGOW
FRENCH AND GERMAN PUBLICATIONS
1992

University of Glasgow French and German Publications

Series Editors: Mark G. Ward (German)
                   Geoff Woollen (French)

Consultant Editors : Colin Smethurst
                     Kenneth Varty

Modern Languages Building, University of Glasgow,
Glasgow G12 8QL, Scotland.

First published 1992.

Printed by Castle Cary Press, Somerset BA7 7AN.

ISBN 0 85261 371 7

CONTENTS

Preface

I am indebted to John Benjamins Publishing Company for permission to reprint material from my book entitled *The Narrative Works of Günter Grass: A Critical Interpretation.* I am also grateful to my colleague Andy Hollis who painstakingly read the text and suggested many improvements.

A special word of thanks is due to Stella Walker and Elaine Kelly who prepared the text for publication.

Noel L. Thomas
Salford

August 1992

CHAPTER I

BIOGRAPHICAL DETAILS

In surveying Günter Grass's life and career it is wise to introduce a note of caution from the outset. Grass's novelle *Katz und Maus* and his novels are not autobiographical but fragments from his own experience; reminiscences and associations fashion the fabric of his prose writings. Grass has made this clear in an interview with Kurt Lothar Tank:

> So weit ich mich auf mein eigenes Leben zurückerinnern kann, finde ich weder in der *Blechtrommel* noch in der Novelle *Katz und Maus* Passagen aus meinem Leben. Ich habe auch nicht die Absicht, etwas Autobiographisches zu erzählen, und glaube auch nicht, daß es möglich ist. Auf der anderen Seite gibt es natürlich Erinnerungen an angedeutete Erlebnisse, die nur aus einem Wort, einem Geruch, einem Anfassen, aus einem Vernehmen vom Hörensagen kommen, und diese Dinge, diese Fragmente von Erlebnissen lassen sich viel leichter in einer Erzählung umsetzen. Dazu kommt noch, daß insgesamt jedes Buch mit allen Nebenfiguren, mit der Landschaft, mit der Auswahl und der Wahl des Themas natürlich ein Stück des Autors ist, ein bestimmtes Stück, und auch eine Selbstentdeckung des Autors bedeutet.[1]

Grass certainly selects the input as do all authors: he determines the choice of characters, the landscape and the themes of his writing. Grass's wish to distance himself from his personal biography is accompanied by his desire to remain in the background, as he himself has indicated in an interview with Geno Hartlaub:[2] 'Ich finde mich als Person nicht so abgrundtief interessant, daß ich mich selbst zum Gegenstand wählen könnte. Bei mir verschwindet der Autor von der Szene.' Grass likes to think that it is not his intention to intervene as a person in the narrative flow of his works. He certainly does not appear as moral arbiter in his major works whether this be in *Katz und Maus*, *Die Blechtrommel* or *Der Butt*. He does not attempt to force a political message upon his reader though we know what his political attitudes are from our reading of his theoretical writings, in particular *Über das Selbstverständliche* and *Der Bürger und seine Stimme*. Art and politics belong in his view to two distinctly separate realms and should be kept apart, as he himself says: 'Kunst mit

---

[1] Kurt Lothar Tank, *Günter Grass*, (Berlin, 1974), p.53.

[2] Geno Hartlaub (ed), *Sonntagsblatt*, (Hamburg, 1.1.1967) - also in Gert Loschütz, *Von Buch zu Buch - Günter Grass in der Kritik*, (Neuwied & Berlin, 1968), p.214.

"Aussage" ist unkünstlerisch'.[3] His detachment is further reinforced by his distrust of all ideology which stems from the corruption to which he and his generation were subjected at the hands of the Nazi propaganda machine.

Though Grass likes to absent himself as an individual from his works, he is the great selector and thereby provokes the reader into thinking within a framework which he determines. His choice is, as might be expected, profoundly influenced by his own upbringing, his career and his background. Günter Grass was born in 1927 in Danzig which at that time was a Free City under the supervision of the League of Nations and was inhabited by a mixed population of Germans, Poles and Kaschubs. It was here, in this place of contact between the Germans and the Slavs, that the war broke out in 1939, a war which was to sever the links between the two linguistic communities, which led to the expulsion of the Germans in 1945, and after which Danzig was renamed Gdansk. Grass uses Danzig, or at least a suburb of Danzig called Langfuhr, as the focal point of *Katz und Maus*, though, of course, the military action takes place elsewhere. In the 'Danzig Trilogy', ie *Die Blechtrommel, Katz und Maus* and *Hundejahre* , Danzig serves as the starting point and remains the centre of attention until 1945 and is regarded by Grass as a microcosm of Germany. This is a justifiable viewpoint in that events in Danzig mirrored the events taking place in Germany proper.[4]

Grass came of mixed parentage, his father being of German descent and his mother belonging to the small linguistic community of the Kaschubs whose language, though distinct from Polish, was of Slavonic origin. This mixed parentage and the multinational population of Danzig contributed to making Grass acutely aware of the tensions which existed between Teuton and Slav. As a result he became especially sensitive to the needs of the Slav peoples and in particular to the wrongs which were committed against the Poles - and the Russians - in the name of Germany. It is not coincidence that the battlefield where Joachim Mahlke is engaged in warfare should be that of Russia. Grass's sympathies made him into an appropriate person to accompany Willy Brandt to Warsaw in 1970 to sign the German-Polish Treaty, which was an attempt to normalize the relations between the Federal Republic and Poland in the wake of the Social Democratic Party's Ostpolitik. One other aspect of the parental influence was the fact that he was brought up as a Roman Catholic and remained so until he withdrew from the Church in

---

[3] *Der Spiegel*, 'Grass: Zunge heraus', 4.9.1963, p.76
[4] H. L. Leonardt, *Nazi Conquest of Danzig*, (Chicago, 1942), p.vii.

1974. He does not, however, view Catholicism as a source of moral influence but regards its greatest strength as being pagan: 'Diese Religion äußert sich im Alltag nicht christlich, sondern heidnisch. Das mag, vom Protestantismus aus gesehen, die Schwäche dieser Religion sein, aber vom Katholiken aus gesehen, auch wenn er nicht mehr glaubt, ist diese kräftige Portion Heidentum eine Stärke'.[5] We should not, therefore, be surprised to find constant references to religious themes in *Katz und Maus* - and also in *Die Blechtrommel* - but it is the heathen, idolatrous aspect of Catholicism which comes into play and not its moral import. The conflict between reason and religion is one which informs *Katz und Maus* as it does many of his other works.

The decisive trauma which had the most profound influence upon Grass's mind was the impact produced by the Hitler era. Without being a National Socialist, he was deeply affected and moulded by the period of the Third Reich, as he himself says: 'Mein Geburtsjahr sagt: ich war zu jung, um ein Nazi gewesen zu sein, aber alt genug, um von einem System, das von 1933 bis 1945 die Welt zuerst in Staunen, dann in Schrecken versetzte, mitgeprägt zu werden'.[6] In the same context he thinks of himself as 'eher das Zufallsprodukt eines halbwegs zu früh geborenen und halbwegs zu spät infizierten Jahrgangs'. Like Mahlke, Grass was infected not so much by the specific political ideas of National Socialism - National Socialism is scarcely mentioned as such in *Katz und Maus* - but by the totality of the emotional climate of the time. He was not aware that his generation was being abused by a criminal regime and believed until the final stages that the war unleashed by Germany was a just one.[7] His experiences during the Third Reich were in many ways typical of those of his age and he likes to think of himself as a representative of his generation: 'Ich wurde im Jahre 1927 in Danzig geboren. Mit zehn Jahren war ich Mitglied des Jungvolkes, mit vierzehn Jahren wurde ich in die Hitlerjugend eingegliedert. Als Fünfzehnjähriger nannte ich mich Luftwaffenhelfer. Als Siebzehnjähriger war ich ein Panzerschütze. Und als Achtzehnjähriger wurde ich aus amerikanischer Kriegsgefangenschaft entlassen: Jetzt erst war ich erwachsen'.[8] Only then did he realise the extent to which the Nazis had exploited his youth; only then did he understand what crimes had been committed in the name of Germany. As a nineteen-year-old he became aware of the guilt the German people had heaped upon

---

[5] Hartlaub, p.215.

[6] Günter Grass, *Über das Selbstverständliche*, (Neuwied & Berlin, 1968), p.169.

[7] *Time*, 13.4.1970, p.74.

[8] *Über das Selbstverständliche*, p.114.

themselves. It is not surprising that guilt was to become one of the central themes which the author Grass 'selects', one which dominates nearly all his prose works, in particular *Katz und Maus*.

Grass served on the Eastern front and saw the destruction of human life that Hitler's war involved. He gives the mathematical details of war in terms of one class of pupils:

> Es waren einmal achtunddreißig Schüler. Alle im Jahre 1922 geboren. Sechsundzwanzig von ihnen wurden im Jahre 1940, acht von ihnen im Jahre 1941 Soldaten. Die restlichen vier zogen, weil sie schwache Augen oder Herzklappenfehler hatten, erst im Spätherbst des Jahres 1944 in den Krieg. Als der Krieg zu Ende war, lebten noch zwölf von den achtunddreißig.[9]

Grass himself was wounded in the fighting near Cottbus in 1945 and recalls one of his own terrifying experiences on the Russian Front in 1944:

> Nach mehrtägigem, sinnlos anmutendem Hin und Her, schließlich nach Absetzbewegungen, geriet die gesamte Kompanie unter Beschuß einer sowjetischen Werferbatterie, auch Stalinorgel genannt. Die Kompanie - Sturmgeschütze und Panzergrenadiere - hatte in einem Jungwald, so hieß es, Bereitstellung gezogen. Der sowjetische Beschuß mag drei Minuten lang gedauert haben. Danach war über die Hälfte der Kompanie tot, zerfetzt, verstümmelt. Die meisten Toten, die Zerfetzten, Verstümmelten waren wie ich siebzehn Jahre alt.[10]

He maintains that his generation was a victim of the heroic concept of death: 'Der Krieg setzte sich nicht zusammen aus Ritterkreuzträger-Histörchen; vielmehr war er der geplante und fortwährende Verschleiß von jungen Menschen, die leben, auf jeden Fall leben wollten und denen jede Möglichkeit des Protestes gegen die demagogische Heroisierung ihres Todes genommen wurde'.[11] He describes how the Iron Cross was regarded as a holy symbol during the Nazi period,[12] how it became the goal of a whole generation and yet was the norm set by a criminal regime: 'Das Ritterkreuz belohnte militärische Leistungen, deren Ziele ein verbrecherisches System gesteckt hatte'. It could be maintained that *Katz und Maus* is the tale of a Knight's Cross awarded to a young man for whom courage in war has become a 'Glücksbegriff' and that it was the reward of a criminal regime for his military achievements.

---

[9] Ibid, pp.13f.

[10] Günter Grass, *Widerstand lernen, Politische Gegenreden 1980-83*, (Darmstadt& Neuwied, 1984), pp.93-4.

[11] See Note 6, p.115.

[12] Ibid, pp.182ff

By the end of the war Grass had been disabused of the Nazi ideology and in the post-war period he became increasingly suspicious of all ideology. In the immediate aftermath of war he worked in a potash mine and then later as a stone mason. His period as a potash-miner completed his rejection of dogmatic politics: 'Weiter lernte ich dort im Kalibergwerk, ohne Ideologie zu leben'.[13]

One other feature of Grass's career is his involvement in politics on behalf of the Social Democratic Party of Germany. Especially in the elections of 1965, 1969 and 1972 Grass was engaged in electioneering on its behalf. Many of the articles in *Über das Selbstverständliche* and *Der Bürger und seine Stimme* are either election addresses or related to these political activities. One issue which emerges in the course of these writings is the German attitude to the past. Grass highlights in particular the German incapacity to come to terms with the events of the past:

> So wie die Bauern im Herbst ihre Futterrüben einmieten, versuchten die redlichen Deutschen ihre Vergangenheit einzumieten. Aber Futterrübenmieten werden im Frühjahr angestochen, dann stinkt es landauf, landab, und keine Idylle ist vor dem vergorenen Anhauch sicher. Die Ungeheuerlichkeit ist nur einen Satz lang: Die Deutschen haben, indem sie es taten, indem sie es zuließen, sechs Millionen Menschen ermordet.[14]

Grass's view that the Germans are much inclined to ignore the bestiality of the Nazi regime is corroborated by commentators such as Rudolf Augstein,[15] who claims that Adenauer behaved as though the first duty of the citizen in the Federal Republic was to forget, and sociologists such as Martin and Sylvia Greiffenhagen,[16] who speak of the devastating ignorance about the period of the Third Reich on the part of pupils in 1976/77. Alfred Grosser, the French historian, describes Germany's relationship to its own history in the following terms: 'Kein anderes Land ist von seiner Geschichte vor 1945 so abgeschnitten, ist so weitgehend konditioniert durch das letzte Vierteljahrhundert' [17] The Germans' fractured attitude to their National Socialist past is also another theme which is in evidence in *Katz und Maus* and one which stems from Grass's own experience of the Third Reich.

---

[13] Ibid. p.72.

[14] Ibid, p.165.

[15] Rudolf Augstein, 'Konrad Adenauer und seine Epoche' in *Die Ära Adenauer*, (Frankfurt am Main, 1964), p.69.

[16] Martin and Sylvia Greiffenhagen, *Ein schwieriges Vaterland* (Frankfurt am Main, 1981), p.59

[17] Alfred Grosser, 1972, quoted in Greiffenhagen, p.39.

It may be stated in conclusion that in writing *Katz und Maus*
Günter Grass the author makes the following selection as a result of
his upbringing, career and background: he picks Danzig as the focal
point of his narrative, chooses characters who belong in the main to
his own generation and in particular those who were involved in
making war on the Eastern front, and highlights specific themes
which stem from his own experiences during the National Socialist
period: guilt, political and social amnesia and Catholicism. As an
author he does not intrude into the narrative flow and is hostile to
the pronouncement of ideological attitudes and rejects ideology as
such. He is concerned rather to reflect the climate of his time, or as
he states in an interview with Manfred Bourrée: 'Ein Schriftsteller
hat nicht das Recht, anzuklagen oder zu verurteilen. Ein
Schriftsteller muß aufzeigen ... ich will nur die Strömungen der Zeit
einfangen'.[18]

---

[18] Manfred Bourrée, *Echo der Zeit*, (Recklinghausen, 18.11.1962), also in Loschütz, pp. 197-8.

CHAPTER II

PROBLEMS OF INTERPRETING *KATZ UND MAUS*

In assessing character and events within a literary work of art the reader is dependent upon information supplied from within the work. At the same time, however, the reader will be consciously or unconsciously aware of happenings which took place in the outside world in the years preceding and accompanying the writing of the work concerned. Such external factors may be mentioned directly or merely hinted at during the course of the narrative. There may be other occurrences which are not referred to in the text but which nevertheless cast their shadow over the work concerned - facts which everyone reading a modern novel or novelle will be aware of without their being mentioned at all. In short, each work of art is the product of the age from which it proceeds and reflects, however dimly, the period of time in which it originates. Each narrative work is encompassed and qualified by factors which derive from the history of the period concerned. Furthermore each work of art is embedded in a cultural tradition to which it owes allegiance. In evaluating *Katz und Maus* the reader draws upon details from the inside world of the novelle, from the outside world of political and social happenings and from the literary continuum to which the work is firmly attached.

Understanding *Katz und Maus* hinges in the first instance on coming to grips with the narrative situation within the novelle. Pilenz, the narrator, tells the story of Joachim Mahlke whose main objective in life ultimately consists in gaining the Knight's Cross. Initially, the reader may regard Pilenz as a narrative device through which Mahlke's life and death are made manifest. The narrator stresses that he has no certain knowledge of Mahlke's character or motivation: 'Nie hörte ich, was er dachte' (p.37), viewing his behaviour as mysterious and enigmatic. At the same time the narrator tries to divert attention from himself - 'doch soll nicht von mir die Rede sein' (p.25). What emerges eventually, however, is the impression that Pilenz is deceitful and untrustworthy, both as a character within the narrative and as a narrator, and that his attitude to Mahlke is flawed. The author Grass for his part does not force any interpretations upon us, and the reader's sense of assurance is never secure. The reader is left considering whether this story does not reveal just as much about the narrator as it does about the protagonist. Ambiguity becomes the hallmark of the narrative

situation and characterizes the relationship between narrator and
protagonist. Martin Swales in his book on the German novelle states
that the characteristic of the German novelle is the articulation of
interpretative ambivalence and he describes it as 'a hermeneutic
gamble, as a tension between an experience and the interpretations,
the readings to which it gives rise'.[1] *Katz und Maus* belongs to this
tradition: the story is constantly open to doubt and its ambiguity and
ambivalence present the reader with fundamental problems of
interpretation, rendering impossible any dogmatic account.

The story of Mahlke and Pilenz is clearly fictional, though as has
been suggested elsewhere it contains fragments from the life and
experience of Günter Grass. There are parallels with the career of
the author: the mere fact that the hero and his creator both see action
on the Eastern Front in the course of the German army's retreat and
defeat in the Soviet Union is enough to confirm this statement. The
world of real happenings exists outside the novelle but is linked to
the narrative by references to actual occurrences in the external
world of reality. The problem which the reader faces in
understanding *Katz und Maus* is gauging the extent to which
extrinsic, factual events should be drawn into consideration in
reaching an appreciation of this work of fiction.

A series of references is made in the narrative to locations which
featured in the course of the Second World War and which no doubt
received a mention in the 'Sondermeldungen' to which Grass was so
accustomed in his youth. The invasion and defeat of France in May
1940 is casually dismissed as the 'goings-on in France' ('dem
Rummel in Frankreich' p.19); the 'Westerplatte', the tongue of land
at the mouth of the Vistula, the bombardment of which from the sea
was the first salvo of the war, is also introduced in passing into the
text (p.33); General Rommel's advances in North Africa and the
German occupation of the Crimea in 1941, which marked the high
point in the German series of successes and the low point in the
fortunes of the Allies (p.99); and nearly all the other place names
which are mentioned in the narrative are either geographical
indications of retreat or names of battles which were stages in the
defeat of the Axis Powers. The fighter pilot who visits the school
narrates his exploits in the Battle of Britain which, like the
engagements in which Mahlke is involved, was lost (see pp 60-62),
and he himself was eventually shot down over the Ruhr in 1943. It is
worth recalling the other heroes whom Mahlke reveres: one is his
father, a locomotive driver who was posthumously awarded a medal
for bravery in saving human life on the occasion of a train accident

---

[1] Martin Swales, *The German Novelle*, (Princeton, 1977), p.40.

(see p.123); and the other is Kommodore Bonte who was awarded the Iron Cross in the battle for Narvik when under attack from British naval units in April 1940. It is not stated in the text that the 'hero of Narvik' was killed in the engagement (p.21). Indeed all Mahlke's heroes are dead.

Allusions to battles are skilfully and sometimes humorously built into the text in a way which does not reveal their military and political significance. The narrator tells us, for example, how Mahlke's mother and aunt have difficulty sorting out their geographical facts:

> Auch Gespräche über die Frontlage - die beiden verwechselten Kriegsschauplätze in Rußland mit solchen in Nordafrika, sagten El Alamein, wenn sie das Asowsche Meer meinten - wußte Mahlke mit ruhigen, nie verärgerten Hinweisen in die richtigen geographischen Bahnen zu lenken: 'Nein Tante, diese Seeschlacht fand bei Guadalcanar statt und nicht in Karelien'. (p.121)

The fact that the battle of El Alamein was, to quote Churchill, 'the turning point in British military fortunes during the War' or that the naval and land battle of Guadalcanal in the Solomon Islands was regarded as a partial American success is ignored, as one might expect in this context. The significance of these battles is masked within the text and the narrator presents them to the reader in meaningless fashion. The same is especially true of the Russian place-names which the reader encounters in the closing stages of the novelle and of Mahlke's life. Before Mahlke takes refuge on the partially submerged minesweeper he meets a group of schoolboys who insist on hearing about his exploits as a tank gunner and tank commander. In particular they want to know whether he destroyed the enemy tanks 'bei Bjälgerott oder bai Schietemier' (p.163) (Belgorod being north of Kharkov and Zhitomir much further to the west, near Kiev). The holder of the Iron Cross has to admit that his military achievements took place on the Western fringe of the Ukraine in the area of Kovel-Brody-Brezany and in Buczacz close to the town of Lvov (p.163). Merely from this brief encounter it becomes clear that Mahlke is accomplishing his deeds of valour for a war machine which is in full retreat and that he is engaged in a senseless war, one which is already lost. This impression is reinforced still further when Mahlke delivers to Pilenz the lecture which he would have given in the school hall. As they row across to the wreck, he describes how he fires on the enemy tanks in his first engagement north of Kursk and then in the counter-offensive near Orel (p.169). Kursk was the scene of the great Russo-German tank battle which, coming a few months after the defeat at Stalingrad, finally sealed the fate of the German army and in which the Germans suffered some 900,000 casualties.[2] Mahlke's bravery is in vain, he is being exploited in a war which in purely military terms has already become pointless. As Alexander Ritter points out, the names of the Soviet towns are 'militärgeschichtliche Schlüsselbegriffe für den Vorstoß der sowjetischen Truppen im Rahmen ihrer Winteroffensive 1943/44 und die verlustreichen Rückzugsgefechte der deutschen Wehrmacht'.[3] This fact is not obvious from the narrative, but only becomes evident when reference is made to works of geography and military history. For Pilenz does not view the exploits of his friend against the background of history and politics. He does not think in strategic terms. It is left to the reader to extract a pattern from the details which are supplied in the narrative by relating them to facts drawn from the outside world. Pilenz is concerned to conceal rather than reveal anything that he might find uncomfortable or disturbing. The readers have to compensate for the narrator's dissembling but they remain unsure as to how far this compensation should go in coming to an understanding of *Katz und Maus*.

The concealment or distortion of reality also figures largely in the two speeches which the air pilot and the U-boat commander deliver in the school hall to the assembled pupils. The air force lieutenant recounts his exploits in a casual, humorous manner, as though he had been engaged in some sort of circus stunt, and flavours his presentation with slang words which also serve to divert attention from the fact that he is involved in acts of killing:

> Gleich beim ersten Einsatz kam uns ein Verband mit Jagdschutz vor die Nase, und das Karrussel, sag ich, mal über mal unter den Wolken, war perfekt: Kurvenflug. Ich versuche mich höherzuschrauben, unter mir kreiseln drei Spitfire, schirmen sich ab, denke, wär doch gelacht, wenn nicht, stoße steil von oben, hab ihn drinnen, und da zeigt er schon Spuren, kann noch gerade meine Mühle auf die linke Tragflächenspitze, als ich auch schon eine zweite im Gegenkurs kommende Spitfire im Visierkreis, halte auf Propellernarbe, er oder ich; na, wie Ihr seht, er mußte in den Bach, und ich dachte mir, wenn du schon zwei hast, versuch es doch mal mit dem dritten und so weiter, wenn nur der Sprit reicht. (p.60)

He concludes his talk in amusing fashion by mentioning, as an extra item, the achievements of the squadron's dog which has learnt to jump by parachute, and describes how one of his colleagues regularly went into action in his pyjamas (pp. 61-62). The

---

[2] John Keegan & Richard Holmes, *Soldiers*, (London, 1985), p.134 & p.141.

[3] Alexander Ritter (ed), *Katz und Maus. Erläuterungen und Dokumente*, (Stuttgart, 1977), p.73.

fundamental features of war are all ignored or belittled - the fear, the killing and the destruction. For this pilot his military deeds are merely an extension of his accomplishments as a sportsman in the schoolyard (p.61).

The second hero who visits the school - the U-boat commander - diverts attention from the bestiality of war by clothing his account in romantic terminology. Instead of enumerating his successful missions he indulges in hyperbole: '... blendend weiß schäumt auf die Hecksee, folgt, eine kostbar wallende Spitzenschleppe, dem Boot, das gleich einer festlich geschmückten Braut, übersprüht von Gischtschleiern, der totbringenden Hochzeit entgegenzieht'. (p.83) He revels in descriptions of nature and even likens his naval expeditions to the voyages of Odysseus (p.85). Both the pilot and the U-boat commander are in effect the servants of the Nazi war-machine and both render the sordidness of war acceptable to the boys by concentrating upon the heroic and idealistic aspects. Like Pilenz they conceal rather than reveal but what they omit is more important than what they mention. They avoid commenting upon Nazi ideology; and the purpose of the war is totally ignored. These heroes, like the boys they infect with their enthusiasm, appear unaware of the fact that they are supporting a criminal regime. They indulge in concealment just as much as does Pilenz and in so doing reflect the atmosphere of the time. It is not difficult for the reader to identify the nature of their diversionary statements. Pilenz's omissions, however, are much more fundamental and present the reader with more substantial problems of interpretation than is the case with the two war heroes. Nevertheless they - Mahlke and the narrator - are victims of self-delusion and provide us with insight into how Mahlke himself was exploited by a murderous regime, the manifestations of which can be observed in their home town.

Danzig may be regarded as a microcosm of Nazi Germany, as has been indicated elsewhere. It was typical of Germany and of the happenings in Germany up to 1945 in that the events taking place there reflect in miniature comparable occurrences in the larger realm of the Reich itself. After the Nazi takeover in 1939 it even managed to acquire in the vicinity a concentration camp of its own, Stutthof by name, thus bearing a likeness to some other areas in Germany. The name of this concentration camp is mentioned in the course of *Katz und Maus* in connection with Oswald Brunies, one of the teachers who was arrested and sent to Stutthof (see p.150). The narrator is keen to stress, however, that he does not intend to go into the details of this sad affair but promises that it will be dealt with elsewhere, not in relation to Mahlke (p.49). Though Grass as a person is acutely aware of the atrocities which were committed in the death camps of Nazi Germany, they do not feature as a theme in *Katz und Maus* (see p.6). Nevertheless the narrator does refer to the pervading stench of corpses in Germany which is only kept in check, he claims, by the smell of onions (see p.119). This stench of death is as much an indication of the casualties of military action as it is of the murder of civilians, Jewish and others, in the Nazi concentration camps. It is an allusion to the huge loss of life which was the result of the German war of aggression. It will be recalled that the Second World War brought about the death of some 55 million people.[4]

The express exclusion of Stutthof and concentration camps in general from the novelle allows the reader to pursue a number of contradictory thoughts. It permits Pilenz to avoid any discussion, direct or indirect, of the individual's responsibility for the slaughter of the Jews, though, of course, he is not thereby absolved from the guilt associated with his involvement in an aggressive war. Pilenz's exclusion of this theme emphasises that *Katz und Maus*, so it could be claimed, is dealing only with one aspect of National Socialist reality. The reader knows from the study of other works of Grass that an account of Oswald Brunies's life has been given in *Hundejahre* and that Stutthof, the killing that took place there and how this came about, form a major theme in this novel. Grass himself has stated that the relationship between *Die Blechtrommel*, *Katz und Maus* and *Hundejahre* is often overlooked and that the novelle was originally part of *Hundejahre* , taking on proportions which allowed it to achieve a separate identity.[5] Accordingly the three works of the 'Danzig Trilogy' may be regarded as complementary and demonstrating their interrelationship may be of assistance in the process of interpretation.

One further question with which we will need to wrestle in coming to an interpretation of Grass's *Katz und Maus* is in what ways the novelle or aspects of it may be regarded as representative. We have already indicated that Danzig can be viewed as mirroring the German scene - political and social - during the Nazi period. As Irène Leonard has suggested, Günter Grass likes to think of himself as a prototype of his own generation, a self-image particularly evident in the electioneering speech from which we have already quoted.[6] He views himself as typical of the generation of Germans

    [4] Martin Vogt (ed), *Deutsche Geschichte*, (Stuttgart, 1987), p.725.

    [5] Heinrich Vormweg, 'Der Berühmte. Heinrich Vormweg besucht Günter Grass' in *Magnum*, Jahresheft 1964, p.47.

    [6] Irène Leonard, *Günter Grass*, (Edinburgh, 1974), p.1.

whose youth was betrayed and exploited by Fascism and who were sent to war before they could come to any awareness of the issues involved. He is representative also of that group of Germans for whom the war brought the loss of their homeland.[7] He stands for those thinking Germans who are horrified by the crimes that were committed in the name of Germany and who feel a sense of guilt even though they did not bring the Nazi regime into being, nor were they able to influence its policy. Günter Grass fell victim to the heroic ideals which infected the Third Reich: 'Tapferkeit, die ausschließlich an militärischen Leistungen gemessen wurde, geriet meiner Generation zum Glücksbegriff'.[8] He was a product of the ideological contamination to which his contemporaries were subjected. Grass portrays himself as exemplifying his own generation but that does not necessarily make the characters in his novelle into representative figures.

Nevertheless critics tend to regard Mahlke and his fate as being not only the case of an individual but as having a more generalised validity.[9] In that Mahlke is unwittingly exploited by the spirit of his time, it would not be difficult to claim that he is symptomatic of a whole generation. However, Mahlke is not the only character in the novelle, though one could easily be tempted into thinking that he is the principal one. It becomes clear, though perhaps not initially, that the prevaricating narrator, Pilenz, is just as revelatory as is Mahlke. The hero may be typical of the generation which was trapped into going to war and perished as a result of it; the narrator is one of the survivors of the war and even though he indulges in pretence - and also perhaps because he does so - tells us something about post-war reality. It is no coincidence that Matern, one of the main characters in *Hundejahre*, also seems congenitally incapable of salvaging facts from the past - he is, for example, extremely reluctant to admit his involvement in a vicious attack on a Jewish friend of his. Likewise Pilenz does not concede that he was influential in affecting the course of Mahlke's life. Equally well he shows no signs of being able to comprehend the fate of Mahlke and his own involvement against the political and social background of the Nazi period and the post-war period. As readers we have to decide which of these two characters is more typical - Mahlke or Pilenz - or whether the social context is more important than the two individuals alone, i.e. whether their attitudes expose German society, pre-1945 and post-1945, to our critical gaze. We shall need to determine whether the novelle

---

[7] Günter Grass, *Widerstand lernen*, (Darmstadt & Neuwied, 1984), p.13.

[8] Günter Grass, *Über das Selbstverständliche*, (Neuwied & Berlin, 1968), pp.182f.

[9] Ingrid Tiesler, *Günter Grass: Katz und Maus*, (Munich, 1971), p.37.

demonstrates the pathology of one or two individuals or the pathology of a whole society.[10]

---

[10] Gerhard Kaiser, *Günter Grass: Katz und Maus*, (Munich, 1971), p.19.

CHAPTER III

AN ASSESSMENT OF *KATZ UND MAUS*

(a) The Novelle

The dust-cover of *Katz und Maus* in its first edition of 1961 provides
- apart from the name of the author and the publishers - at least three
items of information. One of these is the fact that Grass's short
narrative work is or should be regarded as a novelle. The reader will
find that the description of the book as a novelle is entirely correct.
Indeed at one stage in the narration the headmaster produces a
statement which recalls one of the classical definitions of the novelle:
'Unerhörtes habe sich zugetragen' (p.107), reminiscent of Goethe's
definition of the novelle in terms of 'eine sich ereignete, unerhörte
Begebenheit'. The unique events in *Katz und Maus* certainly conform
to this Goethean categorisation. Even though literary historians have
never reached any definitive conclusions about the nature of the
novelle certain features are traditionally associated with it. Grass's
contribution to the history of the novelle incorporates many of these
features: the compactness and conciseness characteristic of nineteenth
century novellen and the concentration upon one specific aspect of a
person's life or development, hence avoiding the broad narrative
sweep expected of the novel. It could also be claimed that *Katz und
Maus* has two 'Wendepunkte' - finding the 'Wendepunkt' has always
been regarded as a standard preoccupation of Germanists. The one
occurs, according to Gerhard Kaiser, when Mahlke recognizes the
Knight's Cross as his particular means of gaining public recognition
(pp.59-60),[1] and the other when he is denied the opportunity of
addressing the school after he has gained this much-coveted
decoration (p.150).
  The narrative situation is also reminiscent of earlier novellen, i.e.
the presence of a narrator within the novelle giving his version of
character and event. The narrator Pilenz tells a story the events of
which take place between summer 1940 and summer 1944, and this
he does at a distance of some fifteen years or more, the year of its
writing being 1960. We are dependent upon Pilenz's attempt at
mediation and this narrative framework soon makes us aware of the
fact that reality and truth can only be attained in a subjective form.[2]
We also come to the realization that the mode of evaluation of the

---

[1] Gerhard Kaiser, *Katz und Maus*, (Munich, 1971), p.30.

[2] Mark Ward, *Der Schimmelreiter*, (Glasgow, 1988), p.18.

protagonist is seriously open to doubt. Volker Neuhaus emphasises
this point in referring to a number of prose works which include
Thomas Mann's *Doktor Faustus* and Alain Fournier's *Le Grand
Meaulnes*: 'in allen genannten Werken präsentiert ein Erzähler alle
ihm relevant erscheinenden eigenen Beobachtungen und Ergebnisse
von Recherchen zu einer Gestalt, über die er selbst kein
abschließendes Urteil gefunden hat und für deren Beurteilung er
deshalb an den Leser appellieren muß'.[3] Mark Ward in his analysis of
Der Schimmelreiter points to the difficulty of coming to a full
understanding of the main character's motivation and claims that
there is no agreed consensus of interpretation.[4] The same applies to
Joachim Mahlke in *Katz und Maus*.

The narrative situation in Grass's novelle is further complicated
by the enigmatic nature of the narrator's character. The reader is left
uncertain about both protagonist and narrator. The reader's
predicament is analogous to the dilemma with which he is presented
in Meyer's *Das Leiden eines Knaben* which we will comment upon
later. *Katz und Maus* is much in keeping with Paul Ernst's
generalisation that 'novellen are stories of remarkable occurrences
that are never fully accessible to human reason and that leave much
room for the workings of inscrutable powers - whether we describe
them as chance, as divine guidance, or as an inner compulsion'.[5]
Pilenz, it could be claimed, is indeed driven on by an inner
compulsion - as is the case in a different way with Mahlke. The latter
even accords with Martin Swales's statement about the Kleistian
hero: 'His inability to accept chance means that he attempts
unremittingly to order (that is, to do violence to) the world around
him'.[6] Pilenz might not be appealing to the reader, as Volker
Neuhaus suggests, to come to an evaluation of the central character,[7]
but by the nature of his narrative he certainly provokes, possibly
unwittingly, his audience into assessing him. In this way the reader is
drawn into the interpretative process, a hermeneutic challenge,
which, as Martin Swales claims, characterizes the nineteenth century
novelle[8] and is equally a distinctive feature of *Katz und Maus*.
Grass's novelle is firmly embedded in the literary tradition of his
forerunners.

It is also a continuation of the nineteenth century novelle in its use

---

[3] Volker Neuhaus, *Günter Grass*, (Stuttgart, 1979), p.68.

[4] Ward, p.21.

[5] Paul Ernst, *Der Weg zur Form*, (Munich, 1928), p.288.

[6] Martin Swales, *The German Novelle*, (Princeton, 1977), p.29.

[7] Neuhaus, p.68.

[8] Swales, p.44.

of symbolism which is a recurring feature of this genre, whether in Annette von Droste Hülshoff's *Die Judenbuche*, Theodor Storm's *Der Schimmelreiter*, Conrad Ferdinand Meyer's *Das Amulett* or Heinrich Kleist's *Michael Kohlhaas*. Sometimes the symbolism is incidental and sometimes it plays a role which is central to the plot, often supplying the title itself. In many novellen symbols may be, as Paul Heyse claims, the specific things that intimate the particular concerns of a given story.[9] *Katz und Maus* is no exception in that this novelle incorporates into the narrative objects of symbolical value which not only serve to draw the strands of the plot together but also highlight significant episodes and motifs in the story. They act as indirect pointers to a subjective mood and intention, as Friedrich Schlegel has suggested.[10] Unravelling the significance of the imagery of cat and mouse is part and parcel of the interpretative challenge to which the reader must respond.

The novelle, so it could be maintained, proceeds from the case of one individual and then attempts to give the event or sequence of events a universal significance. The novelle relates its internal happenings to the external happenings of the time: it links them with the broader implications of the outside world. In this sphere also it is left to the reader to establish these connections for himself: it is part of the interpretative process. In discussing *Der Schimmelreiter* Mark Ward maintains that 'events in the middle of the eighteenth century with which the story deals on the level of content can be seen as analogous to events occurring in the real world of the time at which Storm was writing'.[11] *Katz und Maus*, too, has to be understood within the context of the happenings taking place within the outside world. The internal events are imaginary and yet run parallel to the external events of the time and they may provide some insight into how the real events came into being. At the same time they demonstrate how an individual responds to a situation existing outside (and within) the novelle.

In conclusion it may be said that Grass's novelle corresponds in many ways to what is regarded as being typical of the nineteenth century German novelle: the unusual event(s), the narrative concentration, the 'Wendepunkt', the presence of a narrator and the framework within which he operates, the symbolism, the interpretative rôle of the reader and the relationship between the internal and external world provide evidence that *Katz und Maus* shares in the tradition of this German literary genre. As Martin

---

[9] Paul Heyse in Josef Kunz (ed), *Novelle*, (Darmstadt, 1968), p.68.

[10] Friedrich Schlegel in Kunz, p.40.

[11] Ward, p.49.

Swales states, the complexity of this work does not distinguish it
from its nineteenth-century forerunners.[12]

(b)   The Dust-Cover

The dust-cover is the first contact that the reader makes with *Katz
und Maus*. We have already stated that it indicates that Grass's story
is a novelle. Two further pieces of information are supplied by the
dust-cover, one of them being, as one might expect, the title itself.
We assume from the title that the event or events described in the
novelle will be adequately summarised by the relationship of cat and
mouse. The cat, we all know, enjoys chasing the mouse, not
necessarily because it is in need of food but because it derives
pleasure from hunting down its victim and playing with it, until the
death of the mouse puts an end to the game. The reader will not be
disappointed: the title of the book provides the central imagery
which becomes the framework of the novelle and dominates the
mode of thinking and feeling of the two main characters: the
narrator, Heini Pilenz, a thirty-two-year-old social worker living in
West Germany, and Joachim Mahlke, who met his death or
disappeared in June 1944. Indeed the whole action of the story
proceeds from a boyish prank which the narrator played upon
Mahlke in the summer of 1940 (see p. 6). Pilenz admits reluctantly,
though not initially, that it was he who set a cat onto Mahlke's
Adam's apple, the mouse-like, abnormally large protuberance in his
throat. The cat's attack signals the starting-point for the story, in that
it makes Mahlke aware of his physical inadequacy, and it is this
awareness which serves to motivate his actions. The feelings of guilt
from which Pilenz subsequently suffers force him to become a
narrator: 'Ich aber, der ich Deine Maus einer und allen Katzen in
den Blick brachte, muß nun schreiben' (p.6). The cat's attack has
thus a twofold significance.

At least initially it is clear that the mouse of the title is the
'mouse' in Joachim Mahlke's throat, for his huge larynx is frequently
referred to as a 'mouse'. However, the fact that Pilenz sets a cat onto
Mahlke's throat does not allow one to equate Pilenz with the cat. It
would rather incline one to regard the narrator as being in league
with the cat. Commentators have differed in their attempts to
identify the cat. John Reddick automatically assumes that Pilenz is the
cat, which he describes as an amalgam of Cain and Judas, the
betrayer who tantalizingly hunts down his victim, to whom Reddick

---

[12] Swales, p.58.

ascribes the role of Abel and Christ.[13] Johanna E Behrendt puts forward the opposite view that the cat is not outside but within Mahlke himself.[14] Hans Magnus Enzensberger sees the cat as representing society.[15] Hermann Pongs regards it as fate;[16] while another commentator draws parallels between the cat and the Virgin Mary, who seems on occasions to merge almost indistinguishably into Eve, the eternal temptress.[17] Pilenz's agonized question as to whether there are such things as stories which have an ending (p.133) suggests that stories have a constant, haunting element, but does not exclude the possibility that they may continue in a slightly modified form, and in this instance it even allows the cat to have a shifting identity. Only a close examination will allow the reader to fathom the cat's mysterious identity.

The third piece of information on the dust-cover - the illustration - is yet more ambiguous and ambivalent, though it begins to acquire significance only after the reader has completed the book. The dust-cover of the 1961 edition of *Katz und Maus* shows a large black cat set against a green background. A black Iron Cross is dangling on a red and white ribbon from its neck. Subsequent editions of the novelle retain this picture of the cat with its war decoration - apart from the Rowohlt edition - though the green background is often replaced by a black one. Ultimately the green background of the picture will allow the reader to recall that the schoolboy's prank takes place in the grass of a sports field, that Mahlke's military prowess was demonstrated in the countryside of Russia, and that the hero of the story finally disappears into the hold of a partially submerged minesweeper which is itself surrounded by the grass-green water of the Baltic. Eventually the reader will be inclined to explain the mystery of the dust-cover by recollecting that Mahlke intended to hide in the radio cabin of the ship which he had furnished as though it were a chapel dedicated to the Virgin Mary. At this point the reader may produce a number of statements which are, however, largely conjectural: Mahlke plunges, as it were, into the amniotic sea and, inverting the process of birth, re-enters the womb from which he proceeded; the would-be Christ is re-enveloped by the womb. Cat-like, he haunts the mind of one of the war's survivors; and from

[13] John Reddick, *The 'Danzig Trilogy' of Günter Grass*, (London, 1975), pp.90 and 120.

[14] Johanna E. Behrendt, 'Die Ausweglosigkeit der menschlichen Natur. Eine Interpretation von Günter Grass' *Katz und Maus*', *Zeitschrift für deutsche Philologie*, 87 (1968), 546-62. (Also in Rolf Geißler (ed), *Günter Grass Materialienbuch*, (Darmstadt & Neuwied, 1976)).

[15] Hans Magnus Enzensberger, *Einzelheiten*, (Frankfurt am Main, 1962), p.228.

[16] Hermann Pongs, *Dichtung im gespaltenen Deutschland*, (Stuttgart, 1966), p.36.

[17] Noel L. Thomas, 'An Analysis of Günter Grass' *Katz und Maus* with particular reference to the religious themes', *German Life and Letters*, 26 (1973), 227-38.

beyond his watery grave he dictates in Christ-like fashion the thoughts and feelings of the spellbound narrator. Only detailed analysis of the text can prove or disprove the validity of such statements. However, the illustration does make it clear that it is the cat that gains the Iron Cross and not Mahlke. What is known is that Grass himself designed the dust-jacket - so much is stated at the back of the book. Cat-like, the author plays his little game with the unsuspecting reader. In order to probe the enigma of this illustration let us examine the various aspects of the novelle, firstly, the character of Mahlke, secondly, the character of Pilenz and, thirdly, the relationship between protagonist and narrator. In the process we shall investigate the imagery of cat and mouse and this will contribute to an understanding of the novelle as a whole.

(c)   Joachim Mahlke

Initially one is inclined to concentrate one's attention on Joachim Mahlke, the would-be hero of the story, simply because in the first instance one is prepared to take the words of the narrator at their face value and accept that Pilenz's ostensibly modest desire to remain in the background is genuine and thoroughly credible ('doch soll nicht von mir die Rede sein, sondern von Mahlke oder von Mahlke und mir, aber immer im Hinblick auf Mahlke' [p.25]). Joachim Mahlke is described as being fourteen years old shortly after the beginning of the Second World War. The reader is then presented with the story of Mahlke between the years of 1939 and 1944 when he disappears into the hold of the sunken minesweeper at the age of eighteen. His story is told against the background of the events of the Second World War. Such events take place, however, on the periphery of his consciousness, though preoccupation with his own particular problems may be considered normal for a person of his age. Pilenz even allows him his own time-reckoning, his own B.C. and A.D.: 'Vor dem Freischwimmen, nach dem Freischwimmen' (p.33). If one had to locate his ego, then one might be tempted to situate it in his Adam's apple, for this becomes the focal point of his existence, that pivot around which everything else revolves. Not that his larynx had always played such a dominant role in his life, for, before he learnt to swim, he was a nothing - at least according to Pilenz - a something that nobody noticed (see p.32). He hears of miraculous things about the submerged minesweeper and this goads him on to gain his swimming-certificate. Once he has attained this, he starts to perform various 'miracles' on the ship. He out-swims and out-dives his class-mates and salvages all manner of strange objects from the hold of the ship. He finds down below, for example, a fire-extinguisher, hoists it to the surface and proceeds to spray the sea with foam. By his feats of exhibitionism he soon establishes, according to Pilenz, a legendary reputation for himself. We are told that he wears a variety of articles around his neck ranging from a screwdriver to a tin-opener, and a pendant depicting the Virgin Mary. The narrator maintains that the articles and Mahlke's feats of daring are intended to divert attention from Mahlke's goitre-like Adam's apple. These objects, however, may be regarded as sexual symbols and as such serve to accentuate the Adam's apple as a sign of sexuality rather than concealing it.[18]

In a section which has been referred to as the core of the novelle Pilenz draws together what he considers to be the main elements in his hero's character:[19]

> Eigentlich - mögen später Gerüchte und Handfestes dagegen gesprochen haben - gab es für Mahlke, wenn schon Frau, nur die katholische Jungfrau Maria. Nur ihretwegen hat er alles, was sich am Hals tragen und zeigen ließ, in die Marienkapelle geschleppt. Alles, vom Tauchen bis zu den späteren, mehr militärischen Leistungen, hat er für sie getan oder aber - schon muß ich mir widersprechen - um von seinem Adamsapfel abzulenken. Schließlich kann noch, ohne daß Jungfrau und Maus überfällig werden, ein drittes Motiv genannt werden: Unser Gymnasium, dieser muffige, nicht zu lüftende Kasten, und besonders die Aula, bedeuteten Joachim Mahlke viel, und zwangen Dich später, letzte Anstrengungen zu machen. (p.43)

Here Pilenz seems to make it quite clear what the three decisive elements were in Mahlke's life - though there is some sense of improvisation in the way Pilenz lists these elements: firstly, the Virgin Mary, secondly, his Adam's apple, and thirdly, his old school. A second quotation which may help to indicate the possible political implications of the novelle occurs in Grass's collection of political essays entitled *Über das Selbstverständliche* (1968): 'Das Ritterkreuz belohnte militärische Leistungen, deren Ziele ein verbrecherisches System gesteckt hatte' (p.182).

Let us look first at the quotation from the novelle itself. Pilenz claims that the only woman to whom Mahlke devotes himself is the Virgin Mary. All his actions, whether at school or later in the army, are undertaken with her in mind. Along with the school and his Adam's apple she is one of the principal motive forces within his life. One should not imagine, however, that his adoration of the

---

[18] Kaiser, pp.20f.

[19] Karl Korn, 'Epitaph für Mahlke', *Frankfurter Allgemeine Zeitung*, 7.10.1961. (Also in Gert Loschütz, *Günter Grass in der Kritik*, (Neuwied & Berlin, 1968), p.31).

Virgin Mary stems from a conventional attitude to Catholicism.
Shortly before his disappearance, Pilenz has Mahlke explain the
nature of his beliefs, in particular that he does not believe in God
(p.156). Gusewski, the priest, maintains that Mahlke's worship of the
Virgin Mary borders on pagan idolatry. This is particularly apparent
in the narrator's description of Mahlke stretching out his hands
towards Mary, 'jene überlebensgroße Gipsfigur' with her flat chest
and glass eyes (cf. p.115). What he is idolizing seems, to judge by
Pilenz's statements, something which is hollow, sterile and lifeless,
something which is valueless in its remoteness from life. Despite
these less endearing qualities Mahlke seems attracted to her almost on
a sexual level. Hence Mahlke can state that he does not intend to get
married. Like Oskar and many of the characters in *Die
Blechtrommel*, Mahlke surrenders himself to things, rather than to
people.

How does his devotion to the Virgin Mary manifest itself? Pilenz's
statement - the so-called 'novelle-core' - suggests that Mahlke's feats
as a boy were inspired by the Virgin Mary. The narrator describes
Mahlke's activities on the minesweeper. His constant companions in
his sallies into this underworld are a screw-driver and a pendant
depicting the Virgin Mary. But she, unlike the screw-driver, is
allowed to take part in Mahlke's activities in the gymnasium. She has
to accompany him in all his most daring exercises, whilst the screw-
driver remains in the changing-room. Gymnastics appears to fulfil
the same function in Mahlke's life as diving. Both present him with
opportunities to explore the heights and depths of his existence and
also to impress his fellows. It is also worth remembering that in *Die
Blechtrommel* Christ is described as a gymnast who displays great
athletic prowess in hanging on the cross. Hence one is not surprised
to find later that the Chapel of the Virgin Mary was originally a
gymnasium or that the school's gym itself appears very much like the
inside of a church. Though Mahlke shows great ability both as a
swimmer and a gymnast, the impression is created that he is not able
to cope with ordinary, down-to-earth reality. The spheres of
operation of Mahlke as a boy have their counterpart later on in the
two fields of war associated with the aeroplane and the submarine,
ie. those which are not land-based. The idea that Mahlke is the
equivalent mentally and emotionally of a fish out of water is
suggested later in the novelle when the narrator describes how
Mahlke prays at the altar to the Virgin Mary: 'Auf den Strand
geworfene Fische schnappen so regelmäßig nach Luft' (p.58). Land
is not Mahlke's natural habitat. He is a terrestrial misfit.

The two pendants are intended to serve the same purpose, for

Mahlke wears them ostensibly in order to divert attention from his Adam's apple. In doing so he may, wittingly or otherwise, achieve the opposite effect. The Adam's apple is, however, something more than just a physical deformity which is a source of embarrassment. On the symbolic level it is an indication of his feeling that he is different from his fellows and a sign of his own inadequacy. If one ponders the religious associations of 'Adam's apple', then Mahlke's over-sized larynx is the external manifestation of his own alienation from his contemporaries, a reminder of his own sinfulness. He experiences a sense of original sin, which stems not from an act of doing, but rather from a state of being. Both Mahlke and Oskar in *Die Blechtrommel* are victims of a physical deformity which is the externalization of a state of psychological unbalance.

Mahlke also uses other objects to conceal his Adam's apple. After the war has broken out, Mahlke introduces pompons amongst his school-fellows. Once they have become too popular amongst his friends, Mahlke replaces them by a huge safety pin which is intended to keep a woollen shawl in position under his chin. He makes a final and decisive break with pompons on the occasion of the fighter-pilot's visit to the school. The airman with the much-coveted decoration round his neck relates his war exploits to the pupils in the hall of the school. During the course of the address Mahlke finally removes the pompons from his neck and it is clear from this episode onwards that all his efforts will be concentrated on gaining such a decoration, for only the possession of such a 'Bonbon' (e.g. p.102) can compensate completely for his feeling of inferiority and assuage his sense of discontent. As has been pointed out earlier, this stage in his development may be regarded as one of the two 'Wendepunkte'. The next time a war-hero, in this instance a U-boat commander, comes to the school, Mahlke steals the hero's medal from the gym changing room, unbeknown to his teacher and his class-mates. Pilenz's suspicions, however, are confirmed when he swims out to the minesweeper. Here he finds Mahlke sitting naked on the deck with the war medal dangling by its ribbon from his neck. For the first time Mahlke has found something which can adequately dispel his feelings of inferiority, which, according to Pilenz, can bring his Adam's apple to rest (p.103).

In *Die Blechtrommel* Oskar, the dwarf, likens himself to Christ. In *Katz und Maus* the narrator compares Joachim Mahlke with the person of the redeemer. This comparison does not occur often but it is of sufficient frequency to be of significance. In describing some of the treasured objects in Mahlke's room in the 'Osterzeile' the narrator refers to a stuffed owl in the following terms: 'Auch die

Schnee-Eule hatte den ernsten Mittelscheitel und zeigte, gleich
Mahlke, diese leidende und sanft entschlossene, wie von inwendigem
Zahnschmerz durchtobte Erlösermiene' (p.25).

When Pilenz visits Mahlke on the minesweeper, the latter is
described as having the redeemer's countenance (p.102). On a later
occasion when the narrator observes his hero in church in front of
the altar to the Virgin Mary, he notes his similarity to Jesus (p.114).
Finally when Pilenz encounters the recently-decorated tank-
commander in school, he is once again struck by his Christ-like
facial expression (p.147). Mahlke appears, to judge by the narrator,
to be adapting aspects of Catholic thinking and feeling to his own
needs. He likens himself to Christ and in so doing preserves some of
the outward trappings of Christianity. The trimmings he has retained
are those which serve to satisfy, if not to glorify, his own ego. In
associating himself with Christ, he accentuates the awareness of his
own suffering and throws his own image of himself out of focus.
His striving to emulate Christ is the result of his inability to accept
his own human limitations and imperfections. Mahlke perhaps
suggests that he cherishes this image of himself as the redeemer when
he almost physically assaults one of his class-mates for having drawn
on the board a picture of him complete with halo and a Christ-like
expression of suffering (p.45), though it may be that he objects also
to the blasphemous nature of the drawing.

There is a special significance in the fact that Mahlke does not
believe, so the narrator claims, in God. Joachim Mahlke comes to an
awareness of himself and his special physical peculiarities as he
enters puberty. He leaves the years of unknowing and of innocent
harmony behind. He frenetically searches for an appropriate fig-leaf
to cover his physical - and psychological - nakedness. It is not
coincidence that when Pilenz visits him on the minesweeper he finds
him sitting naked on the deck dangling the stolen Knight's Cross
from his neck - and Mahlke even tries to dangle it in front of his
genitals (p.104). For Mahlke the military decoration is the ultimate
fig-leaf, the one which allows his fragmented mind to recover its
original harmony. A number of references to harmony and
symmetry occurs throughout the text (see p.41, p.103, p.128, p.147).
One particular reference is especially telling: the Knight's Cross is
described as 'proclaiming symmetry as a creed' (p.103). Whilst his
schoolmates sun themselves on the deck of the minesweeper, Mahlke
in his role of Adam and would-be Christ labours to atone for his
sense of disproportion: 'Mahlke machte es sich nicht leicht: wenn wir
auf dem Kahn dösten, arbeitete er unter Wasser' (p14). His feats are
miracles of over-achievement: he feels compelled to over-

compensate for his physical - and psychological - inadequacies. The first Adam wishes to become a second Adam. He wishes to attain salvation, to achieve wholeness. He wishes to bring redemption to the world, but the only world of which he is aware is the inner world of Mahlke. His quest for redemption is an act of spiritual self-abuse because it is turned in upon itself. Nevertheless he still pursues the goal of purity, the aim of liberating himself from all inconsistencies and paradoxes. He still wishes to redeem himself. Accordingly - so one concludes - he views himself as the son and lover of the Virgin Mary and hence cannot believe in Christ or for that matter in God, for both of them cannot be allowed to exist in his world since they would be rivals for the Virgin's favour.

The acts in which Mahlke indulges are for the most part senseless - though this would not be unexpected from a person whose behaviour is still that of an adolescent. Spraying the sea with foam from a fire-extinguisher is a particularly good example of an action which, though entertaining and impressive, fulfils no purpose (p.10), and which has incidentally sexual overtones. Playing a gramophone, which he has recovered from the hold of the ship, without a record is equally pointless (p.27). His masturbatory feat has the same air of futility. This is emphasised most trenchantly by the fact that the seagulls devour his seed. Only they benefit from his act of giving.

What he does achieve by his feats is that he focuses attention upon himself, he plays to an audience and gains their approval, or on occasions arouses their disgust. Mahlke's independence, his identity even, relies on confirmation by others, whether this be the Virgin Mary, his own schoolmates or the school-assembly, the latter being his ultimate goal. As Pilenz states, 'ich kann und will nicht glauben, daß Du jemals auch nur das Geringste ohne Publikum getan hättest' (p.58). For Mahlke actions also serve the purpose of proving his superiority: diving for objects in the hold of the ship, masturbation and his heroics on the field of battle all have this as their aim. Ingrid Tiesler comments on this central feature of his behaviour: 'Für Mahlke hat die Tat vor allem den Wert des Sieges über andere, das heißt, sie dient der Erhöhung des Selbstwertgefühls auf Kosten anderer'.[20]

Mahlke is portrayed as part of an unproductive cycle. The gulls eat his life-giving sperm in the same way that they snap up the boys' sputum which consists of the masticated remains of the birds' droppings. All this takes place on the wreck of a ship which is gradually rotting away and whose superstructure is covered with rust and gulls' excreta. The children's cycle of infertility has its

---

[20] Ingrid Tiesler, *Günter Grass: Katz und Maus*, (Munich, 1971), p.62.

counterpart in the nominally adult cycle of death and destruction: the fighter-pilot engages in the Battle of Britain - a battle which is lost - and shoots down enemy planes only to be shot down himself over the Ruhr in 1943 (p.62). Mahlke's orgy of killing on the Russian front is ultimately followed by his own non-resurfacing - or non-resurrection - from the hold of the ship. This roundabout of death and destruction is reinforced in particular by the stench of corpses which pervades the whole of Germany during the war years (p.119). This is not to maintain that Mahlke is incapable of altruism - he does rescue one of the schoolboys from drowning (p.68) and his removal of the contraceptive from the door handle of the classroom may also belong to the category of acts which proceed from a consideration of others, though Mahlke does enjoy the approbation which he thereby receives (p.28). However, as Irène Leonard points out, Mahlke's sensitivity in the private sphere does not extend to the public sphere.[21] And even his ostensibly selfless acts achieve the effect of putting his classmates in their place and of demonstrating his distinctiveness. Destructiveness and sterility assume a more dominant role in the novelle than positive features of human behaviour during the years in which the action takes place.

The senseless peculiarity of his actions above all provokes the admiration of his classmates and their approval stimulates him still further: 'Aber gerade das Sinnlose und bewußt Zerstörerische des tagelangen Umzugspiels bewunderten wir, ...' (p.74). Mahlke's exploits on the minesweeper prepare him for the amoral deeds in the arena of war. The visits of the fighter-pilot and U-boat commander also prepare the Knight for the gladiatorial deeds which will earn him the award of the Cross. The two talks achieve a twofold effect: they make him aware of the supremacy of the Knight's Cross over all the other much-prized fig-leaves, and divert his mind from the reality of war, on the one hand by the description of war as a sport, and on the other hand by clothing war in romantic terminology. Mahlke has reacted to a schoolboy's prank in a humourless, egocentric manner and sets forth for the field of battle, not, however, having outstepped the confines of the childish perspective. He seeks military distinction through acts of destruction, as Johanna Behrendt states.[22] In another sense, however, Mahlke reduces the conflict to what it is - a senseless game. The schoolboy in uniform (cf. p.150) cannot accept the inconsistencies of his own inner world, wishes to attain wholeness and be released from suffering and sets out to achieve this by acts of unwholesome destruction. Mahlke, the

---

[21] Irène Leonard, *Günter Grass*, (Edinburgh, 1974), p.29.

[22] Behrendt, p.119.

Saviour, suffers from the delusion that he may gain redemption without his having any meaningful relationship with others, for the only 'people' who have any relevance for his life are the flat-chested, glass-eyed Virgin Mary and his dead father. Ultimately, because his own internal world is out of joint, he turns mindlessly to the destruction of the external world. Only because his mind remains diverted from reality is he capable of going to war, almost unaware of the implications of his actions. The letters he sends to his mother and aunt highlight the nature of his puerile behaviour. He sends them drawings of Russian tanks, which with childish precision are marked with a cross as a sign that he has 'bagged' them (pp.131-133). On a later occasion Pilenz speaks of the Knight's Cross as 'jener eiserne Artikel, der das kindliche Kritzeln und Durchkreuzen so vieler russischer Panzer zu belohnen hatte ...' (p.160).

The hero recounts his over-achievement in war to Pilenz, the narrator, as the latter rows him across to his underwater chapel. He claims that the Virgin Mary appeared to him in battle. She was accompanied not by the Christ-child but bore instead the picture of his father and the fireman in front of their locomotive just before they died attempting to save the lives of others (pp.169-79). She placed the photo over her stomach. Mahlke had only to direct his fire at the picture to ensure a direct hit on the tank. Not only was he destroying the tank - and presumably the occupants - but he was also ejaculating a stream of deadly shells at the Virgin whilst at the same time symbolically killing his father. He is a superman of war; he performs the ultimate in over-achievement, killing enemy, Virgin Mary and father simultaneously. In attempting to reintegrate himself, to attain a state of purity, he annihilates all that he claims to value most. Now the Christ-child, who has impregnated the Mother of God with his deadly sperm, demands the acclamation which is his due. However, he is refused admittance to the school hall, that paradise which has been the goal of all his endeavours and where he hoped to demonstrate his prowess as a military superman.

Having reached the threshold of salvation he is thrust back into a world which is bereft of meaning. Denied the delights of paradise and denied release from suffering, the hero reacts yet again in a self-centred manner to the blow which he has received. So rigid is his obsession with self-healing that he is trapped in the thorny labyrinth of his own mind: 'Aber der Große Mahlke befand sich in einer Allee, ähnlich jener tunnelartig zugewachsenen, dornenreichen und vogellosen Allee im Schloßpark Oliva, die keine Nebenwege hatte und dennoch ein Labyrinth war' (p.154). The military superman yet again turns superchild. The pseudo-Christ finds that he cannot save himself. He turns his back on a reality which he has in any case never understood. His experiences have not led him to self-knowledge. His final trick as a clown (cf p.23) is to dive on a Friday, bearing the Knight's Cross before him, into the hold of the minesweeper, thereby rejoining the Virgin Mary whom he has destroyed in battle. Since that Friday there has been no Sunday on which Mahlke has resurfaced, though the narrator in his self-delusion does not appear to exclude this possibility of resurrection.

Mahlke is motivated by a mixture of ideals which complement each other in their effect. He is spurred on by the external trappings of Catholicism, though the moral content of Christianity has left little or no mark upon his mind. Certainly he is inspired by the example of his father whose heroism saved the lives of others. However, he is unable to make a distinction between the two types of heroism, as Volker Neuhaus observes: 'Der Sohn bemerkt nicht die Wert-verschiebung zwischen dem Menschenleben rettenden Heldentum des Vaters und dem eigenen Heldentum, das sich gerade in der Vernichtung von Leben äußert und keine der Instanzen, die die Aufgabe hätten, ihn zu leiten, ist imstande, ihn darauf aufmerksam zu machen'.[23] Remnants of the knightly deed as military achievement and as a form of religious homage are present in his act of firing at the enemy tanks.[24] He is goaded on by the vision of the Knight's Cross and not the swastika. He is the equivalent of the National Socialist superman even though he does not give any evidence of allegiance to Nazi ideology and even though he voices some reservations about what he describes as 'diese Überbetonung des Soldatischen' (p.116). Mahlke seeks to remedy his sense of disharmony by acts of destructiveness which exclude all elements of altruism. Thus he is exploited by the criminal regime whose ideals he is unwittingly supporting and he performs actions the purpose of which he does not question.

His deeds are presented as being based upon a desire for self-realization rather than for the improvement of the world. Accordingly Mahlke exemplifies the description of the Germans which Clawdia Chauchat produces in the course of Thomas Mann's *Der Zauberberg*: 'Aber es ist bekannt, daß ihr um des Erlebnisses willen lebt. Leidenschaft, das ist Selbstvergessenheit. Aber euch ist es um Selbstbereicherung zu tun. C'est ça. Sie haben keine Ahnung, daß das abscheulicher Egoismus ist, und daß ihr damit eines Tages als Feinde der Menschheit dastehen werdet?'[25] Mahlke's quest for self-

---

[23] Neuhaus, p.77.

[24] Tiesler, p.61.

[25] Thomas Mann, *Der Zauberberg*, Book II, (Stockholm, 1946), p.384.

enrichment has as its outward manifestation the need to demonstrate his superiority vis-à-vis his contemporaries. He is dependent upon their affirmation of his prowess. Once he is denied their approbation in the school hall, once public recognition of his success is withheld, his infantile world is unable to withstand this shock and he retreats into childishness - not even the approval of the Virgin Mary is sufficient to compensate him for this rejection. By committing suicide he fulfils the prophecy which his classmates made: 'Der hängt sich irgendwann mal auf oder kommt ganz groß raus oder erfindet was Dolles' (p.77).

(d) Pilenz

If one views the novelle solely in terms of the character of Mahlke, then the reader might readily accept Johanna E. Behrendt's thesis that the cat which traps Mahlke is within Mahlke himself. His desire to outstrip his schoolmates and to outshoot his rivals, whether they be his father or the Virgin Mary, this godless behaviour stems from an innate sense of inadequacy. His yearning to emulate Christ leads to his superhuman achievements. Schiller's dictum 'In deiner Brust sind deines Schicksals Sterne' could easily apply to Mahlke. However, if one judges Mahlke's story in the light of the narrator's remarks, then another version of the 'truth' may begin to emerge. Indeed many commentators would wish to qualify Schiller's words and regard Pilenz, the narrator, as the person who is the guilty one and who helped to drive Mahlke to his death. In other words they would shift the emphasis and claim that Pilenz makes Mahlke aware of his inadequacy and goads Mahlke on to over-achievement in life - and in death - in the sense that Mahlke continues to dominate Pilenz's mind even after his disappearance.

One aspect of Pilenz, the narrator, emerges at an early stage in the novelle: Pilenz is not the most reliable of narrators. As Ingrid Tiesler states, 'alles, auch die Handlungsverknüpfungen und die zitierten Aussprüche Mahlkes, trägt das Signum dieses unzuverlässigen Berichterstatters'.[26] Even with regard to the central event in Mahlke's life, Pilenz is reluctant to state quite unambiguously what did in fact happen. When he first mentions this incident, he supplies three possible versions of the truth: 'So jung war die Katze, so beweglich Mahlkes Artikel - jedenfalls sprang sie Mahlke an die Gurgel; oder einer von uns griff die Katze und setzte sie Mahlke an den Hals; oder ich, mit wie ohne Zahnschmerz, packte

---

[26] Tiesler, p.49.

die Katze, zeigte ihr Mahlkes Maus: und Joachim Mahlke schrie, trug aber nur unbedeutende Kratzer davon' (p.6). In the next line Pilenz accepts responsibility for having placed the cat on Mahlke's neck, but does so in such a grandiose manner that one almost has the impression that he is attaching too much significance to this action - and for that matter to himself. Pilenz prevaricates not only about the cat's attack on Mahlke. There are many other instances of the narrator's equivocation. He suffers or pretends to suffer from lapses of memory: he is unsure, for instance, about the facial appearance of Mahlke (p.44). There is uncertainty as to whether Mahlke introduced pompons to his part of Germany or whether they were his own invention (p.47). He sometimes describes imaginary conversations as though they did take place (p.110). He is unsure, so he maintains, of whether he is restructuring the past in the light of the present (see p.82 and p.27). Statements are made only to be followed by a correction, which does not enhance the narrator's credibility (p.151). There are other occasions when the narrator makes statements the validity of which he destroys by the subsequent introduction of a subjunctive (p.157).

However, he also tells untruths, sometimes of a fundamental nature; this is especially so in the hours before the hero's disappearance. For example, he lies about the length of time he has hired the boat (p.171). After obtaining some food Pilenz returns to Mahlke and maintains that the authorities have been asking about him on two occasions - though this is clearly in conflict with a previous statement. Then he goes on to claim that Mahlke's mother has already been arrested (p.167). Such lies allow Pilenz to enjoy a feeling of superiority. For one brief, but decisive, moment in his life he can take pleasure in the fact that he is now on top: now he can kick physically (p.168) and psychologically the person on whom he has lavished so much love and - on occasions - so much hate.

The distortions and falsehoods which Pilenz produces achieve a twofold effect: they make the reader adversely disposed towards the statements the narrator makes and in a perverse sense they draw attention to the personality and motives of the narrator. Perhaps they even incline the reader to think that such an untrustworthy biographer is unlikely to have come to a proper understanding of the person he feels impelled to write about. Pilenz is at pains to emphasise that the story he is telling is about Mahlke and not about himself (p.25). The over-insistent desire on the part of the narrator to remain in the background makes the wary reader suspicious and encourages questions concerning Pilenz's motives.

The way in which the narrator presents himself also inclines the reader to view Pilenz's statements with caution. As Gerhard Kaiser points out, the narrator is not only conscious of the fact that he is telling an imaginary tale but he also knows and makes it clear that he is an invention of the author.[27] He refers to his own artificiality: 'Der uns erfand, von berufswegen, zwingt mich, wieder und wieder Deinen Adamsapfel in die Hand zu nehmen, ihn an jeden Ort zu führen, der ihn siegen oder verlieren sah ...' (p.6). Elsewhere he raises the question yet again as to who placed the cat on Mahlke's neck whilst at the same time throwing doubts on his own role as narrator or narrating device: 'wenn ich nur wüßte, wer die Mär erfunden hat, er oder ich oder wer schreibt hier?' (p.122). He even describes his literary confession as a kind of artistic game: 'Zwar ist es angenehm, Artistik auf weißem Papier zu betreiben ...' (p.105). All such occasions - as well as Pilenz's insecure grasp of the truth - reduce the narrator's credibility and provoke the reader into adopting a questioning attitude towards him.

Pilenz is obviously full of admiration for Mahlke, though his admiration degenerates into horror and disgust from time to time (p.77). He becomes a zealous altar-boy at communion so that he can peer down Mahlke's collar and see the various objects dangling from his neck (p.30); he picks up Mahlke from his home so that he can accompany him to school (p.101); and it is Pilenz who coins the title 'Der Große Mahlke' in order to describe his hero and the admiration he feels for him (p.97). This admiration borders on idolatry almost in the same way that Mahlke idolises the Virgin Mary (p.115). He is certainly obsessed by him, not only during the war years, but after his death as well. Many examples can be found of how Pilenz cannot rid his mind of thoughts of his hero. For instance, he describes how when he sets out to visit friends or acquaintances in post-war Germany, he is 'immer noch auf dem Weg zu Mahlkes Mutter und Mahlkes Tante, zu Dir, zum Großen Mahlke' (p.118; see also p.65; and p.156). He cannot, for example, clear his mind of recollections of his last trip across the water to the submerged minesweeper: 'Obgleich ich nie mehr und bis heute nicht in ein Ruderboot stieg, sitzen wir uns immer noch gegenüber ...' (p.168). His obsessive preoccupation with Mahlke, the constant presence of Mahlke in his mind, is made unmistakably clear in the frequent retrospective conversations he conducts with Mahlke and in the way he often addresses him directly, as though he were relating the story on occasions to Mahlke himself. Such situations seem to emphasise the nightmarish quality of a bad conscience: 'ich schwimme langsam in Brustlage, sehe weg zu vorbei, zwischen Resten der Entlüfter

---

[27] Kaiser, pp.7f.

hindurch - wieviel waren es eigentlich? - sehe, bevor meine Hände
den Rost fassen, Dich, seit gut fünfzehn Jahren: Dich!' (p.102). The
circumstances of previous encounters with Mahlke reimpose
themselves constantly upon Pilenz's consciousness without his being
able to banish their intensity. He is incapable of controlling these
invasions from the past. The passage of time - he is writing as we
know fifteen years after the events of his youth - does not diminish
their immediacy.

Pilenz's feelings for Mahlke seem to be of a near-claustrophobic
intensity. Possibly they stem originally from the fact that Pilenz is
attracted to his hero simply because the object of his veneration is so
decisive. Occasionally the reader is aware that Pilenz's hero-worship
is tinged with homosexuality. Perhaps it is no coincidence that Pilenz
maintains that he and his former classmates cannot remember the
appearance of Mahlke's upper lip and think that they might be
confusing Tulla Pokriefke with Joachim Mahlke (p.44). Perhaps
there is significance in the fact that the narrator tries to oust thoughts
of Mahlke by thoughts of Tulla who ironically is in any case a
somewhat masculine girl (p.99): 'Während ich schwamm und
während ich schreibe, versuchte und versuche ich an Tulla Pokriefke
zu denken, denn ich wollte und will nicht immer an Mahlke denken'.
Pilenz's worship of his hero also extends to Mahlke's sexual organ
which he describes as being 'viel erwachsener gefährlicher
anbetungswürdiger ...' (p.40). It is certainly true to say that Pilenz,
by his own admission, does not make any headway with the ladies.
To suggest that Pilenz's hero-worship is tinged with a homosexual
element would make much of the narrator's behaviour
comprehensible, though his behaviour is adequately motivated even
without this potentiality.

Indeed Pilenz does not provide any clear-cut indication of the
possibility of his own homosexual tendencies. Given the fact that he
is always inclined to conceal rather than reveal himself, such a
confession would be highly improbable. Furthermore he will be
cognizant of the fact that an admission of this kind could have had
serious if not fatal consequences for him during the Nazi period, as
Ingrid Tiesler points out.[28] The theme of homosexuality is introduced
into the novelle by the behaviour of the priest Gusewski, or rather
by Pilenz allowing Gusewski to be exposed as having homosexual
leanings (see pp.112-3).

What is nevertheless clear is that Pilenz suffers from a guilt
complex. Initially, however, it is not obvious what the nature of his
guilt complex is. He explains to us that he feels himself to be under a

---

[28] Tiesler, p.89.

compulsion to write. Pater Alban takes over the role of father-confessor and Pilenz relates to him the story of Mahlke, of cat and mouse and what he describes as 'mea culpa' (p.101). On another occasion he refers to his guilt and says that he would not have felt the need to write if Mahlke had hidden the medal below the deck of the minesweeper, or if he and Mahlke had not been friends (p.104). It is Pater Alban who suggests that Pilenz should get the whole thing off his chest by writing (p.125). In giving this advice the priest uses the term 'sich freischreiben' which suggests the idea of 'writing one's way to inner freedom'. A similar though more common term - 'sich freischwimmen' -is employed to describe Mahlke's efforts to pass his swimming-test and at the same time to swim his way to freedom. Such an expression conveys the idea of getting away from parental or similar supervision and of finding one's feet, presumably in the adult sphere. Both Mahlke and Pilenz, it could be claimed, suffer from a feeling of alienation, from a sense of inadequacy. Both lack the capacity to maintain their minds in a state of equilibrium, they have difficulty keeping matters in perspective, and neither of them has managed to tread the road of freedom from adolescent preoccupation with self to the establishment of a meaningful relationship with others and with the outside world in general.

Let us return to our original problem. What is the specific basis for Pilenz's guilt complex? Pilenz does commit at least four acts which would be sufficient to justify, retrospectively, a troubled conscience. Firstly, it is he who suggests amongst other things that Mahlke could hide on the minesweeper (p.162) after having denied him the possibility of Gusewski's assistance (see pp. 160-1); secondly, though he reminds Mahlke to take the tin-opener with him before the latter dives into the hold, it emerges afterwards that Pilenz had put his foot on it and had finally thrown it away (pp.174-5); and thirdly, Pilenz does not return to the boat on the evening of the same day (p.176). Above all else, of course, Pilenz places the cat on Mahlke's neck, and thereby sets in motion the chain of events which leads eventually to Mahlke's disappearance. He also indulges in symbolical actions which imply that he is not loath to be rid of Mahlke and which reveal at least an aspect of Pilenz's attitude to his so-called friend: for example, Pilenz wipes the drawing of Mahlke as a redeemer off the blackboard (p.45); he removes his hero's name and favourite sequence contained in the 'Stabat mater' from the wooden partition of a latrine (p.138); the altar boy, Pilenz, celebrates the Last Supper with his Saviour (p.159); and finally - a symbolical act like the throwing away of the tin-opener - he packs the photograph of Mahlke's father and of the locomotive at the bottom of his bag which he ultimately loses in the fighting near Cottbus (p.177).

The narrator's actions and his lies certainly reveal him at least as a traitor in attitude. He acts out the role of Judas to Mahlke, the would-be Christ, as Gerhard Kaiser suggests.[29] He is the false friend. He takes his revenge in emotional terms on a person who at least ostensibly is the epitome of masculinity, who has been an object of veneration for him, but who disregards his admiration. It is almost as though he kills the thing he loves. Perhaps he can brook no rivals, perhaps he is jealous of the Virgin Mary, of Mahlke's father and of Tulla Pokriefke.

Pilenz contributes to Mahlke's downfall in two ways: firstly, he aggravates his hero's innate hypersensitivity and feeling of inadequacy by placing the cat on Mahlke's throat and thus helps to condition his response to the shock of not being allowed to speak in his school hall; and, secondly, he inclines Mahlke to think of suicide by telling him lies about the arrest of his mother and the arrival of the men who are looking for him. He is guilty of creating an atmosphere of mind which plays upon Mahlke's weaknesses. In this sense Mahlke is a relatively blameless though rather mindless victim, whilst Pilenz justifiably suffers from a troubled conscience. It is clear, however, that in his obsessive sense of guilt Pilenz is concerned primarily about his own self and the state of his own mind. He is not really concerned about the person or fate of Joachim Mahlke. His objective is to purify his own mind. He seeks peace of mind with the same degree of intensity with which Mahlke attempted to cleanse his mind from imperfection. Both pursue aims which are in essence amoral and egocentric.

It could also be maintained paradoxically that Pilenz appears to revel in his constant breast-beating. His guilt complex becomes the main motivation within his life. He tells us, for example, that he has taken up a poorly paid job as a social worker, more or less in order to assuage his restless conscience (p.138). Remove Pilenz's guilt complex and his character would soon lose its focus, in much the same way that Mahlke's mouse and his attempts to satisfy it form the substance of his being. Mahlke conforms to the climate of his time by playing the hero and hence unwittingly supports a criminal regime, in the same way that Pilenz feels it his duty to suffer from a guilt complex because of his involvement in Mahlke's downfall.

The guilt complex to which Pilenz is so fervently attached has indeed many strange aspects. He fails to come to terms with the past and hence cannot establish a healthy relationship with the present. This inability stems in essence from the fact that his preoccupation

---

[29] Kaiser, p.15.

with his own self blocks his avenue of approach to reality. Behind shuttered windows both Mahlke and Pilenz engage in emotional self-abuse. Mahlke, the superchild, sets out for the playground of war in Russia and is but dimly aware that war involves killing. His war game expresses itself in childishly drawing tanks and crossing them out. Pilenz is also blissfully unaware of the destruction of human life which is caused by Mahlke's quest for wholeness and Mahlke's preoccupation with his own ego. The narrator dismisses the invasion of France as the 'Rummel in Frankreich' (p.19); and he is equally offhand about the German occupation of the Crimea and Rommel's activities in North Africa (p.99). Pilenz, the narrator writing after 1959 (see p.177), has not outgrown his original childish attitude. Like his hero he is concerned not about the killing that was war, but about the superman's downfall, and more particularly about whether he, the narrator, may be justified in viewing himself as blameless. Like Mahlke, he is a do-it-yourself redeemer who operates exclusively on his own home territory. He is sorry for himself but not for others. He has made self-pity into the supreme law within his own walled city. He is a victim of moral blindness. By the end of the narrative Pilenz has not even achieved his objective. He set out to deliver himself from his troubled conscience, to cleanse himself from guilt through the act of writing. He singularly fails to realize his aim and it might even be claimed that he merely aggravated his condition. Both narrator and hero may be viewed as failures.

(e) The imagery of cat and mouse

In the closing paragraphs of the novelle Pilenz describes how what began with cat and mouse still torments him today. We have no reason to doubt his word. The narrator is haunted by the vision of Mahlke's disappearance, of what in German could be referred to as 'Untergang' which has the double meaning of going down (ie diving) and of downfall. Mahlke haunts him from beyond his watery grave. This first Adam conditions the narrator's attitudes and responses in the present but, unlike the second Adam, he offers no respite to his suffering, he cannot heal his tormented soul. Pilenz may have acted the betrayer in Mahlke's life, he may have played the cat to Mahlke's mouse. However, in Mahlke's after-life Pilenz is certainly no longer the cat and he cannot even switch roles. Only if Mahlke were to resurface, would Pilenz gain release from his torment, for such a resurrection would provide proof that Pilenz did not bring about Mahlke's downfall. This is a vain hope and it is a sign of Pilenz's lack of realism that he attends meetings of those survivors who gained a Knight's Cross during the war, imagining that he might see Mahlke there (pp. 177-8).

Pilenz may be regarded as the cat in Mahlke's life, particularly if we view him as the representative of the group attitude towards Mahlke. On the other hand it must be admitted that Mahlke would not have proved susceptible to the schoolboy's prank and fallen victim to the all-enveloping atmosphere of National Socialism, had he not possessed some innate weakness. In any case, if Mahlke's larynx is equated with the mouse, in other words if the mouse sticks in his throat, then this would even suggest that Mahlke can indeed be considered to be the cat. Be that as it may, Pilenz is not the cat in Mahlke's after-life. Over fifteen years after the disappearance of Mahlke, it is Mahlke who stalks Pilenz. The narrator is pursued also in a slightly different way. He is trapped on the one hand by the person of Grass as author within the novelle into telling Mahlke's story and he is compelled on the other hand by his own 'guilty' conscience to write the biography of a person who during his life might have been Pilenz's victim. In trying to assuage his conscience he adopts in effect the role of Mahlke's evangelist, as Volker Neuhaus suggests.[30] The picture of the black cat as drawn on the dust-cover of the novelle looks down from the wall of Pilenz's mind and plays its game with the mouse below. Gerhard Kaiser aptly describes this reversal of roles in the course of the novelle in the following terms:

> Mahlke ist der Adamsapfel, der Pilenz, trotz aller Schluckversuche, im Halse steckengeblieben ist und immer stecken bleiben wird ... Pilenz, der 'widersinnig aber versessen' nach Joachim Mahlke sucht (p.145), ist zugleich der, der ihn nicht loswerden kann (p.137). Er wird gejagt vom toten Mahlke, er wird mit Hilfe des toten Mahlke gejagt von dem Erzähler, der ihn erfand, er ist der Adam des letzten Autor-Gottes der Erzählung, die Maus dieser Katze, eine Maus, die von ihrer Geschichte umgetrieben wird, weil Pilenz sie als seine Geschichte nimmt und damit überhaupt erst zu seiner Geschichte macht.[31]

During the novelle the cat and the mouse have had no fixed abode, they have had a shifting identity. However, by the close of the story, Pilenz has lost all claim to the title of cat, and he is still pursued by Mahlke. He is a failure on at least two accounts: he has been unable to assuage his guilty conscience and though he has made every attempt to conceal rather than reveal his true identity and his motivation, he stands exposed at the end of the narrative as an unreliable purveyor of information and as the person who more than

---

[30] Neuhaus, p.81.

[31] Kaiser, p.39.

anyone else bears much of the blame for the downfall of Joachim Mahlke.

(f)   Social and Political Relevance

It could be claimed that *Katz und Maus* belongs to the tradition of schoolboy stories such as C F Meyer's *Das Leiden eines Knaben* or Musil's *Verwirrungen des Zöglings Törleß*.[32] In Meyer's novelle a number of adults plays significant roles in the action whether this be the narrator, the King, the Jesuit teacher or the father of the boy. In the story of Mahlke - and this is one of the features which distinguishes it from Meyer's schoolboy story - the adults have a purely peripheral function. There is nobody who acts as a counterweight to the childishness of the schoolboys. Mahlke's mother and aunt do not affect the course of the action - they constantly defer to the boy and thereby enhance his sense of self-importance. They certainly do not promote the process of his maturing. Father Gusewski wants to help Mahlke at one crucial stage in life, i.e. shortly before he retreats into the hold of the minesweeper. However, Pilenz blocks this offer of assistance (see pp. 160-61). The two representatives of the armed forces, the Air Force pilot and the submarine commander, though ostensibly adults, may be considered as not much more than overgrown schoolboys and in effect they encourage his egocentricity. Pilenz the narrator, who in terms of age is obviously adult, has not outstepped the limitations of the adolescent mentality, has no sense of moral awareness and is still trapped in the irresponsibility of a youth. He is afflicted by a blindness which prevents him seeing, fifteen years after the events, the extent to which he has been implicated in them. He is incapable of realizing how political and social circumstances have exerted an influence upon his and Mahlke's lives. A world in which adults and responsible people are absent is portrayed in *Katz und Maus* by an individual who is stunted in moral and emotional terms and has remained irresponsible.[33]   As Gerhard Kaiser indicates, history is presented 'als Exzeß von Umweltsblindheit, gemacht von Bewußtlosen'[34] Pilenz is the vehicle through which the group pressure is brought to bear upon Mahlke: he unwittingly makes Mahlke into a victim and agent of a criminal regime. Günter Grass has stated in one of his interviews that the story of Mahlke exposes church, school, heroism

---

[32] Kaiser, p.35.

[33] Kaiser, p.40.

[34] Kaiser, p.31.

and indeed the whole of society.[35] The reader will readily see the applicability of this statement to the novelle. Some critics, for example Johanna E Behrendt, try to establish a close relationship between Mahlke's career and the history of National Socialism:[36]

> Dieser historische Kriegsweg des Dritten Reiches entspricht sinngemäß Mahlkes eigenem Lebensweg, der von siegreichen und heldenhaften Überleistungen mit darauf folgendem Untergang geprägt ist. Mahlkes Vorgeschichte bis zum Schwimmenlernen aber weist auf die Vorgeschichte und Voraussetzung des nationalsozialistischen deutschen Staates hin und deutet an, daß Mahlke nicht nur diesen, sondern den deutschen Nationalstaat überhaupt versinnbildlicht.

Though reminiscences and correspondences do exist between Mahlke's and Germany's history, identifying him with the German state does not seem justified on the basis of the text itself.

Even though Pilenz proves to be an unreliable narrator and even though all his statements about Mahlke are qualified by this realisation, they both emerge as individuals who have only a partial understanding of their own situations. Both of them view their own lives and problems in purely personal terms: private considerations overrule public considerations. Mahlke engages in war in order to compensate for what he considers to be his own deficiencies. He is not inspired by any sense of allegiance to the ideology of the political movement and the state which he is serving, nor is there indication that he has any understanding of the political realities of the time. In his mindlessness he is exploited and corrupted by a criminal regime which awards the Knight's Cross to those who achieve military distinction in the pursuit of its aims (cf quotation from *Über das Selbstverständliche*). The fact that his humanity is degraded in this way is an indictment of the educational system, institutionalised religion and the community to which he belongs. In the last resort it could be claimed that even he cannot be absolved from blame, but in his defence it must be stated that he is still an adolescent at the time of his death. Pilenz, on the other hand, is viewing the events of his youth from a distance of 15 years. The passage of time should allow a more balanced perspective, but it does not occur in this instance. Pilenz still regards the past in exclusively subjective terms. His viewpoint is still characterised, so it appears, by the immaturity of the adolescent. His mind is blinkered by the insistent desire to rid himself of his feelings of guilt. His preoccupation with his own personal problems ensures that he is unable to establish a relationship between the private and the public spheres. Like Mahlke, he is

---

[35] Reddick, p.158.

[36] Behrendt, p.122 (in *Materialienbuch*).

amoral and apolitical. He is incapable even of benefiting from hindsight. He fails in his attempt to cleanse his mind of guilt and he fails to come to terms with the past. Guilt in itself does not guarantee a realistic assessment of the past. If Mahlke's behaviour implies criticism of 'church, school, heroism and indeed the whole of society', then Pilenz's attitudes are obliquely condemnatory of post-war German reality.

In conclusion, it is interesting to return to a discussion of the dust-cover of *Katz und Maus*. As we have already noted, it is the cat that has been decorated with the Iron Cross on the dust-cover. Since, however, the cat has a shifting identity, the conclusions the reader may reach are ambivalent but in many ways complementary. The cat - and the person of the narrator - stimulate Mahlke into pursuing a career of military distinction leading to the award of the Knight's Cross. This in turn brings about his downfall at the hands of the headmaster - and his ultimate death. Mahlke then turns into the cat and haunts Pilenz. On each occasion it is the cat that emerges victorious and deserves the decoration, but the cat is not a single, constant individual but rather an amalgam of those forces within society to which individuals fall prey.

Chapter IV

THE RELATIONSHIP OF *KATZ UND MAUS*
TO *HUNDEJAHRE*

Günter Grass likes to think of *Die Blechtrommel, Katz und Maus* and *Hundejahre* as forming a unity and he considers that four common elements link the books of the 'Danzig Trilogy' together:[1] firstly, the narrators' feeling of guilt; secondly, the place and time; thirdly, what Grass chooses to call 'die Erweiterung des Wirklichkeits-verständnisses: das Einbeziehen der Phantasie, der Einbildungskraft, des Wechsels zwischen Sichtbarem und Erfindbarem'; and fourthly, the fact that each book is an attempt to conjure up the past, an attempt 'ein Stück endgültig verlorene Heimat, aus politischen, geschichtlichen Gründen verlorene Heimat, festzuhalten' (pp. 10-11). Elsewhere Grass has stated that *Katz und Maus* was originally part of *Hundejahre* and that it finally took on an independent identity of its own, developing into a separate work in its own right.[2] Given their common origins it is particularly illuminating to compare these two narrative works.

Both works centre on Danzig and both works deal with the National Socialist era and with the war. *Hundejahre* specifically refers to events which are intended to belong to the post-war period. *Katz und Maus* does not include any happenings after 1945 apart from the meeting of decorated 'heroes' in 1959. Since, however, the events contained within the novelle are related fifteen years after the incidents themselves, the book provides insight into the post-war attitude of the narrator and is not simply dealing with episodes from the war. In this sense the post-war years are just as much a part of the novelle as are the years of the war.

It is indeed true to say that all the narrators in the 'Danzig Trilogy' write out of a sense of guilt 'aus verdrängter Schuld, aus ironisierter Schuld, im Fall Matern aus pathetischem Schuldverlangen, einem Schuldbedürfnis heraus'.[3] As these words suggest, the nature of the guilt complex is not identical in each of the three works. In *Die Blechtrommel* Oskar is too young to be held directly accountable for the events of the novel and in any case his identity is masked by ironic, satiric and grotesque elements. He is closer to being a narrative device than a literary character. In *Katz und Maus* the grotesque is much reduced in scope and the

---

[1] Heinz Ludwig Arnold (ed), *Günter Grass. Text und Kritik*, (Munich, June 1978), pp.6-11.

[2] Günter Grass in Geno Hartlaub, 'Wir, die wir übriggeblieben sind ...' in Gert Loschütz (ed), *Günter Grass in der Kritik*, (Neuwied & Berlin, 1968), p.214.

[3] Arnold, pp.10f.

imaginative is kept within the confines of the psychologically
feasible. The reader can thus detect the essence of Pilenz's guilt and
at the same time appreciate the narrator's incapacity to relate the
personal to the political, to see himself and others in the context of
his own time. In *Hundejahre* guilt is yet again a dominant theme.
Like *Die Blechtrommel* the novel is divided into three books, with
each part, however, being written by a different narrator. The first
book, 'Frühschichten', is related by Brauxel, alias Amsel, who is of
Jewish extraction, and it deals with the period from 1917 to the birth
of Tulla Pokriefke in 1927; the second book, 'Liebesbriefe', is
narrated in the form of so-called love letters written by Harry
Liebenau to Tulla and covers the years from 1927 to 1945; and the
third book, entitled 'Materniaden', has as its narrator Walter Matern,
whose task it is to handle the post-war years. The central theme of
the novel is the relationship between Jew and German and the central
event is the brutal assault which Matern, amongst others, launches on
Amsel, his blood-brother.

The three narrators can be differentiated one from another in
terms of the quality of their memory. Amsel's memory is active and
inaccurate; Matern's memory is sluggish and recalcitrant; whilst that
of Harry Liebenau is retentive and in many spheres comprehensive,
though he is capable of distorting and suppressing facts, especially in
instances in which his conscience is troubled. Amsel is constantly
observing people and situations and is of an artistic temperament,
whilst at the same time being a contradictory character. His task in
life is to remind Matern of the act of brutality which he committed
against his blood-brother. For him narration is a form of confession
and he tries to provoke Matern into a narrative confession. Harry
Liebenau's prevarications and treachery remind the reader of Pilenz.
Both of them are incapable of establishing meaningful connections
between facts, and of relating their personal experiences to the
broader spectrum of their social and political environment.
Theoretical considerations block Liebenau's thinking and allow him
to overlook the bestiality of the Nazi treatment of the Jews, though
he likes to blame Tulla for the contamination of his mind. His role is
largely passive. Walter Matern, on the other hand, is addicted to
violence. Whereas Amsel thinks with his head, Matern thinks with
his fist. Initially he defends his blood-brother against attack but
subsequently leads the assault on him. In both instances violence is
the characteristic feature of his behaviour. In the post-war period he
is keen to act out the role of judge and conducts a campaign of
vengeance against his contemporaries, quick to recognise the mote in
their eyes but oblivious of the beam in his own eye. Matern cannot

clear his mind of a latent sense of guilt and like Pilenz he is tormented by his fixation on his friend. Both Pilenz and Matern are initially guilty of acts of aggression, and the two aggressors ultimately become subservient to their original victims. The hunter becomes the hunted, or to use the imagery of the novelle, the cat and the mouse exchange roles. Pilenz and Matern both indulge in a similar symbolical act of treachery: Pilenz conceals and then throws a tin opener into the sea, whilst Matern throws a penknife, a present from his blood-brother, into the River Vistula. As Volker Neuhaus suggests, the three narrators of *Hundejahre* incorporate three different ways of viewing the past: 'Opfer, Zeuge, Täter'.[4] This is certainly the case in the first instance, but Matern, the physically orientated individual, soon becomes Amsel's servant and the more he struggles to rid himself of his underlying sense of guilt, the more the culprit falls under the spell of his intellectual superior. Amsel, the editor-in-chief, makes Matern's subservience plain by describing him in the following terms: 'Er geriet in Abhängigkeit. Amsel machte ihn zum Paslack. In kurzatmigen Revolten versuchte er auszubrechen. Die Geschichte mit dem Taschenmesser war solch ein ohnmächtiger Versuch; denn Amsel blieb ihm, so kurzbeinig dicklich er durch die Welt kugelte, immer voraus' (p.72). In *Hundejahre* the reader is presented with three perspectives; in *Katz und Maus* there is only one. In the novelle all the information is channelled through the one and only narrator. As Albrecht Goetze maintains, the narration in Hundejahre is relativized - placed in perspective - by the presence of the three authors.[5] Even though Amsel is an enigmatic individual, he does supply the reader with a set of criteria by which the events and characters can be assessed. He is indeed the only character in the 'Danzig Trilogy' who performs this function. All the other narrators in the 'Danzig Trilogy' are thoroughly untrustworthy as purveyors of information and may easily lead the unsuspecting reader astray. Pilenz is, in effect, an amalgam of Liebenau and Matern: all three of them have something to hide; like the would-be historian Liebenau, Pilenz has no historical sense, no capacity for reaching out beyond the confines of his own ego; and though he likes to think of himself as a passive individual - he calls himself the 'great hesitator' (p.136) - he initiates the action by placing the cat on Mahlke's neck, an act which has its counterpart in Matern's assault on Amsel. The two blood-brothers are interdependent. Two events bind them together - Matern's throwing the knife into the river and the assault which he

---

[4] Neuhaus, p.86.

[5] Albrecht Goetze, 'Die hundertdritte tiefunterste Materniade' in A. Goetze and G. Pflaum (eds), *Vergleichen und Verändern. Festschrift für H. Motekat*, (Munich, 1970), p.276.

and his comrades launch against Amsel. Treachery and violence condition their relationship. Comparable events link Pilenz and Mahlke together - the cat episode and Pilenz's advice to his friend to take refuge on the minesweeper, coupled with the subsequent jettisoning of the tin-opener. As a result both Matern and Pilenz are obsessed subconsciously by the wrongs they have committed and yet intellectually reluctant to admit their guilt. Both are incapable of self-appraisal and neither of them comes to terms with the past. Pilenz still imagines that Mahlke could resurface at a meeting of war heroes in 1959 and hence release him from his suffering, whilst Matern towards the end of the book demonstrates his impenitence by throwing the penknife for a second time into the Vistula. Neither of them has a sure grasp of reality; neither of them achieves self-knowledge. Of the three narrators in *Hundejahre* it could be maintained that Amsel sees and understands, Liebenau sees but does not understand and Matern neither sees nor understands. Pilenz certainly does not achieve any sense of self-awareness and comprehends neither himself nor events. Both works, *Hundejahre* and *Katz und Maus* deal with the problem of 'Vergangenheits-bewältigung', the perceived German failure to come to terms with the past, and the need to recognize and accept responsibility for past actions. The fundamental difference between the two books is that the presence of three narrators in *Hundjahre* allows the juxtaposition of different attitudes to the past and that one of these narrators assists the reader in the task of interpretation, whereas in *Katz und Maus* no such form of orientation exists and the reader is left very much to his own devices.

It can also be maintained that a further significant difference between *Hundejahre* and *Katz und Maus* (and indeed *Die Blechtrommel*) is the fact that the novel ends on a mildly optimistic note in comparison with the earlier novel and the novelle. In *Hundejahre* Amsel tries to subject Matern to an educative process: he attempts to jolt him out of his complacency, for example, by escorting him through the thirty-two chambers of the underground scarecrow hell. The scarecrows are intended to reflect in distorted form Matern's own shortcomings and transgressions. Even though Matern does throw away the knife again, Eddi Amsel refuses to give up, he remains true to his mission in wanting to initiate his friend into a process of reform.

Katz und Maus and *Hundejahre* show similarities in their extensive use of imagery throughout the narrative, and this employment of objective correlatives is a feature of more or less all of Grass's narrrative works. To be reminded of this fact one merely needs to look at the dust-covers of his works with their array of living creatures - cat (the mouse does not appear, presumably having been already swallowed), dog, snail, flounder and rat - and of other objects - the drum for example - equally pregnant with meaning. Grass objects to the use of the word symbolism to describe the presence of the imagery of *Katz und Maus* - presumably because he wishes to stress the external reality of the objects concerned.[6] Nevertheless Grass's incorporation of significant objects into his novelle is very much in line with the symbolism traditionally associated with the German novelle. The dominant symbols in Storm's *Der Schimmelreiter*, Meyer's *Das Amulett* and in Droste-Hülshoff's *Die Judenbuche* have much in common with the imagery which Grass employs in *Katz und Maus*. It is interesting to note, however, that the use of imagery is not confined to Grass's novelle but is a feature of virtually all his novels. In this sense it could be maintained that Grass is not adhering specifically to a tradition of the German novelle in his handling of what the majority of us would tend to think of as symbols but is employing rather what for him is a characteristic mode of expression.

Even if one disregards the dust-cover of *Hundejahre*, it is clear that the dog, like the cat and mouse in the novelle, is a central image within the novel. Parallels are constantly being drawn between the dog and the Hitler regime. Events in the life of the dog are being placed side by side with events which are connected directly or indirectly with Hitler. The increasing bestiality of the Nazi regime is suggested in terms of the dog. The treacherous malice and evil of Tulla are conveyed through the medium of the dog's behaviour. One particularly devastating illustration of how Tulla is represented as having the habits of a dog can be seen in the episode in which she goes to live with the dog, crawling on all fours, barking like a dog, eating the dog's food and resisting all attempts of her parents to persuade her to return home (pp.168-80). Not only Tulla but her brothers and Harry eat the dog's meat and, as though it were some nauseating communion, the act of eating becomes a sign of their spiritual bondage (p.170). One is reminded of Mahlke's ostentatious and equally nauseating consumption of frog's legs, a tin of which is salvaged from the hold of the submerged Polish minesweeper. In the post-war period Matern is accompanied by the dog as he launches himself into a campaign of vengeance in West Germany. The dog's presence is a constant metaphorical reminder of the past and serves as a sign that the German mentality has not yet changed. The imagery in *Katz und Maus* and in *Hundejahre* is part of the narrative

---

[6] See *Life*, 58, 22, p.51.

texture and acts as a cohesive element. At the same time it provides
an insight into the modes of feeling and thinking of the characters
concerned and shapes their behaviour. In this, imagery and episode
contribute to the extension of the reader's understanding of reality,
thus illustrating the significance of Grass's comparison of the three
works of the 'Danzig Trilogy'.

The three narrators of *Hundejahre* may be compared, as we have
already suggested, in terms of the quality of their memory. At the
same time the three of them assume a representative function, for
Liebenau and Matern are a reflection of the German population at
large. As John Reddick states,

> it is one of the novel's driving themes that the horrors of the National
> Socialist years were made possible, at any rate partly, because the mass
> of Germans were predisposed not to see reality as it substantively was,
> but to register it in terms of some received and false notion that rendered
> them effectively blind.[7]

Harry Liebenau ironically agrees with this statement, whilst being
unable to see its applicability to himself: 'Vergessen wollen alle die
Knochenberge und Massengräber, die Fahnenhalter und
Parteibücher, die Schulden und die Schuld' (p.427). Like Harry
Liebenau, the German populace wished to indulge in a collective act
of amnesia. Matern also shares in this general tendency, the desire to
start afresh, to make the year 1945 into the year zero, as though the
past had never existed. Like the dog, the two co-authors seek a new
master in West Germany (see p.427). The dog finds Matern, whilst
the two narrators are engaged by Amsel. Both are impenitent and yet
in their subconsciousness an uneasy conscience makes itself dimly
felt. In their forgetfulness and blindness they are emblematic of
German attitudes to the past. Amsel also refers to the Germans'
inclination to erase the past from their memories: 'Ach, wie sind sie
geheimnisvoll und erfüllt von gottwohlgefälliger Vergeßlichkeit! So
kochen sie ihr Erbsensüppchen auf blauen Gasflammen und denken
sich nichts dabei' (p.646). In *Hundejahre* the coexistence of three
narrators allows the reader to reach conclusions about their
representative function with relative ease. In *Katz und Maus* the
reader is dependent upon the one voice of a single narrator, but close
scrutiny of the text reveals that Pilenz suffers from the same mental
blockage and the same blindness as do Liebenau and Matern in
Hundejahre. Accordingly, the reader comes to the conclusion that
Pilenz also reflects a general trend in post-war German
consciousness.

---

[7] Reddick, p.227.

CONCLUDING REMARKS

As has been suggested earlier, *Katz und Maus* belongs to the tradition of the schoolboy story such as C F Meyer's *Das Leiden eines Knaben*. In both instances the reader is presented with a story which is recounted by a narrator present within the novelle, Pilenz in *Katz und Maus* and Fagan in *Das Leiden eines Knaben*. In Grass's novelle the narrator is a fellow schoolboy who tries to obscure his narrative purpose, whereas Fagan makes his aim quite clear. Pilenz tries to cleanse his mind of guilt whilst Fagan wishes to convince the King of the dangerous character and intentions of his Jesuit confessor. Both narrators, the one pursuing an egocentric and childish objective, the other trying to perform an educative task, fail to achieve their goals. The world of *Katz und Maus* is the realm of schoolboys, school and schoolboy attitudes, and the narrator does not outgrow this domain even fifteen years after the war. Meyer's novelle is populated by adults who determine the tragic outcome of the story. The adults - Hitler and his henchmen - who set the stage for Mahlke's downfall exist outside the novelle, whereas the dominant political figures in the period of French history described by Meyer - King Louis XIV, Madame de Maintenon and their entourage - are present in the narrative. Both boys, Mahlke and Julian, suffer as though in imitation of Christ's passion: Mahlke is crucified in the pursuit of the Knight's Cross, whilst Julian, we are told, is 'schuldlos wie der Heiland' and his experience with his tutors is described as 'das Golgatha bei den Jesuiten'. The two novellen thus incorporate religious associations and references. Both protagonists are presented as pursuing heroic ideals. Mahlke seeks to acquire military distinctions, scarcely aware of the criminal nature of the regime he is supporting; whereas Julian dies in his final delirium with the name of the King on his lips, blissfully and ironically ignorant of the support his sovereign accords to the boy's Jesuit tormentors. Neither boy has any understanding of the generality of the political situation in which each lives and dies.

Fagan's story is a savage attack upon the Jesuits and a denunciation of society, even if the narrator ultimately fails to achieve his objective. Grass's novelle is equally well an indictment of society, though the critical onslaught is much more wide-ranging than is the case in *Das Leiden eines Knaben*. Pilenz and Mahlke are by implication presented as being incapable of coming to terms with reality. Mahlke does not comprehend his relationship to the political environment of his time, whilst Pilenz, even with the ostensible advantage of fifteen years' hindsight, does not understand Mahlke's

predicament nor has he any insight into his own guilt. Both
protagonist and narrator fulfil a representative role: Mahlke stands
for the youth of Germany whose lives were exploited and degraded
by a bestial regime, whilst Pilenz, along with his schoolfriends, acts
as the instrument whereby Mahlke's weaknesses can be abused. In
this way he becomes the vehicle through which the criminal designs
of the regime are transmitted to his - and the regime's - victim.
Pilenz is not shown as benefiting from his attempt to recreate the
past. In this sense Pilenz's story is a narrative - and moral - failure.
Fagan's narration is perhaps doomed to miscarry in advance since
the Edict of Nantes was revoked in 1685, some fifteen years before
the death of Julian. Fagan is preaching against the Jesuits at the time
when their position in society is presumably unassailable. Fagan's
message falls on deaf ears, perhaps because Louis XIV regards art as
a source of entertainment rather than possessing an educative
function. Le Roi Soleil is morally deaf; Pilenz and Mahlke are
morally blind. In *Katz und Maus* the reader is provoked into
directing his gaze at two individuals both of whom could be
considered as being pathological, whilst the society to which they
belong, both Nazi and post-war, can be viewed as being equally
diseased. In reading the novelle one is reminded of Grillparzer's
remark that the novel is psychological, the novelle psychopathic.[1]
Fagan's narration - and the lack of reaction on the part of the king -
raise serious doubts about the quality of French society, even though
it was witness to a cultural flowering in the seventeenth century.
Both novellen reach out beyond the fate of one single individual and
can be viewed as attempts 'to interpret the unusual event or sequence
of events in the context of a generality of human affairs and their
understanding'.[2]

The broad canvas against which both novellen are set contributes
to the difficulty the reader experiences in coming to an evaluation of
the narratives concerned. We constantly ask ourselves which events
and trends external to the novelle cast their shadow over the internal
happenings and what radiation proceeds from the inner world of the
narrative to the outside world of reality. The ambivalence of the
imagery in *Katz und Maus* aggravates the problem of interpretation
still further. It is as though the reader is a spectator at a literary duel
between the two contestants of Mahlke and Pilenz, their shifting
fortunes as victim and victimizer constantly providing food for
thought and assessment. The task of the reader is compounded still

---

[1] Franz Grillparzer, *Sämtliche Werke*, ed. P. Frank and K. Pörnbacher, (Munich, 1964), III, 292.

[2] M. Swales, *The German Novelle*, (Princeton, 1977), p.56.

further by the unreliability of the narrator. Such factors all impose an active role upon the reader, who is dragged willy-nilly into the interpretative process. The participation of the reader as the ultimate judge and arbiter is just as essential in assessing this novelle as it is in *Das Leiden des Knaben* and other German novellen. In attempting to cope with this 'hermeneutic challenge' the reader is faced with a number of interpretations which may be regarded as complementary rather than exclusive.

In assessing *Katz und Maus* the reader will quickly come to the conclusion that it forms an integral part of Grass's literary output and has close associations with other narrative works, especially *Hundejahre*. At the same time he or she will be made aware of the fact that Grass's novelle is deeply embedded in the tradition of the nineteenth-century German novelle. It has been maintained that the latter is provincial, though this label can scarcely be applied to *Das Leiden eines Knaben*, and that this feature has denied it European acclaim. The typical characteristic of the narrative works which have gained recognition in Germany since the Second World War - whether they be those of Grass, Böll, Lenz, Walser or Thomas Mann's Doktor Faustus - is that they are germanocentric. *Katz und Maus* is no exception to this general trend. Perhaps this can scarcely be expected otherwise after the traumatic experience of the German catastrophe. All the post-war writers are engaged in an educative process. In his novelle Grass provides no evidence of any change in the German mentality - at least from the perspective of 1961, the year of its publication. Let us hope that Grass's encoded message does not fall on deaf ears, as did Fagan's narrative attempt.

Narrative Works of Günter Grass

Die Blechtrommel, 1959

Katz und Maus, 1961

Hundejahre, 1963

Örtlich betäubt, 1969

Aus dem Tagebuch einer Schnecke, 1972

Der Butt, 1977

Das Treffen in Telgte, 1979

Kopfgeburten oder die Deutschen sterben aus, 1980

Die Rättin, 1986

Unkenrufe, 1992

All the above works are published in hardback by Luchterhand, Darmstadt and Neuwied apart from his most recent novel which is published by Steidl Verlag, Göttingen.

In quoting from *Katz und Maus* I have used the hardback edition published in 1961 by Luchterhand. The same page-numbering is employed in the Heinemann edition published in 1971 and edited by H.F. Brookes and C.E. Fraenkel. In quoting from *Hundejahre* I have used the hardback edition published in 1963 by Luchterhand.

Suggestions for Further Reading

Behrendt, Johanna E, 'Die Ausweglosigkeit der menschlichen Natur. Eine Interpretation von Günter Grass' *Katz und Maus*', in *Zeitschrift für deutsche Philologie*, 87 (1968), 546-562. (Also in Geißler, Rolf (ed), *Günter Grass Materialienbuch*, (Darmstadt & Neuwied, 1976))

Brode, Hanspeter, *Günter Grass*, (München, 1979)

Kaiser, Gerhard, *Günter Grass - Katz und Maus*, (Munich, 1971)

Keele, Alan Frank, *Understanding Günter Grass*, (Colombia, South Carolina, 1988) (suitable only for general reading)

Leonard, Irène, *Günter Grass*, (Edinburgh, 1974)

Reddick, John, *The 'Danzig Trilogy' of Günter Grass*, (London, 1975)

Neuhaus, Volker, *Günter Grass*, (Stuttgart, 1979)

Ritter, Alexander (ed), *Günter Grass - Katz und Maus*, (Stuttgart, 1977)

Tiesler, Ingrid, *Günter Grass - Katz und Maus*, (Munich, 1971)